Battered by high seas and a northwesterly gale, two German U-boats on patrol in mid-Atlantic meet unexpectedly in the winter of 1941. The chance encounter surprised both boats, which had been fighting the storm for over a week. Journalist Lothar-Günther Buchheim, sent on patrol with the U-96 (in foreground), took this picture evoking the perilous life of Germany's sea wolves.

THE BATTLE OF THE ATLANTIC

Other Publications:

THE SEAFARERS
THE ENCYCLOPEDIA OF COLLECTIBLES
THE GREAT CITIES
HOME REPAIR AND IMPROVEMENT
THE WORLD'S WILD PLACES
THE TIME-LIFE LIBRARY OF BOATING
HUMAN BEHAVIOR
THE ART OF SEWING
THE OLD WEST
THE EMERGENCE OF MAN
THE AMERICAN WILDERNESS
THE TIME-LIFE ENCYCLOPEDIA OF GARDENING
LIFE LIBRARY OF PHOTOGRAPHY
THIS FABULOUS CENTURY
FOODS OF THE WORLD
TIME-LIFE LIBRARY OF AMERICA
TIME-LIFE LIBRARY OF ART
GREAT AGES OF MAN
LIFE SCIENCE LIBRARY
THE LIFE HISTORY OF THE UNITED STATES
TIME READING PROGRAM
LIFE NATURE LIBRARY
LIFE WORLD LIBRARY
FAMILY LIBRARY
   HOW THINGS WORK IN YOUR HOME
   THE TIME-LIFE BOOK OF THE FAMILY CAR
   THE TIME-LIFE FAMILY LEGAL GUIDE
   THE TIME-LIFE BOOK OF FAMILY FINANCE

Previous World War II Volumes:

Prelude to War
Blitzkrieg
The Battle of Britain
The Rising Sun

WORLD WAR II · TIME-LIFE BOOKS · ALEXANDRIA, VIRGINIA

BY BARRIE PITT
AND THE EDITORS OF TIME-LIFE BOOKS

THE BATTLE OF THE ATLANTIC

Time-Life Books Inc.
is a wholly owned subsidiary of
TIME INCORPORATED

Founder: Henry R. Luce 1898-1967

Editor-in-Chief: Hedley Donovan
Chairman of the Board: Andrew Heiskell
President: James R. Shepley
Vice Chairman: Roy E. Larsen
Corporate Editors: Ralph Graves, Henry Anatole Grunwald

TIME-LIFE BOOKS INC.

Managing Editor: Jerry Korn
Executive Editor: David Maness
Assistant Managing Editors: Dale M. Brown,
Martin Mann, John Paul Porter (acting)
Art Director: Tom Suzuki
Chief of Research: David L. Harrison
Director of Photography: Robert G. Mason
Planning Director: Philip W. Payne (acting)
Senior Text Editor: Diana Hirsh
Assistant Art Director: Arnold C. Holeywell
Assistant Chief of Research: Carolyn L. Sackett

Chairman: Joan D. Manley
President: John D. McSweeney
Executive Vice Presidents: Carl G. Jaeger (U.S. and
Canada), David J. Walsh (International)
Vice President and Secretary: Paul R. Stewart
Treasurer and General Manager: John Steven Maxwell
Business Manager: Peter G. Barnes
Sales Director: John L. Canova
Public Relations Director: Nicholas Benton
Personnel Director: Beatrice T. Dobie
Production Director: Herbert Sorkin
Consumer Affairs Director: Carol Flaumenhaft

WORLD WAR II

Editorial Staff for The Battle of the Atlantic
Editor: William K. Goolrick
Picture Editor/Designer: Thomas S. Huestis
Text Editors: Thomas H. Flaherty Jr., Anne Horan
Staff Writers: Richard W. Flanagan,
Henry P. Leifermann, Sterling Seagrave
Researchers: Jane Edwin, Barbara Fleming,
Clara Nicolai, Robin Richman
Editorial Assistant: Dolores Morrissy

Editorial Production
Production Editor: Douglas B. Graham
Operations Manager: Gennaro C. Esposito
Assistant Production Editor: Feliciano Madrid
Quality Control: Robert L. Young (director),
James J. Cox (assistant), Michael G. Wight (associate)
Art Coordinator: Anne B. Landry
Copy Staff: Susan B. Galloway (chief),
Margery duMond, Victoria Lee, Florence Keith,
Celia Beattie
Picture Department: Dolores A. Littles,
Barbara S. Simon

Correspondents: Elisabeth Kraemer (Bonn);
Margot Hapgood, Dorothy Bacon (London);
Susan Jonas, Lucy T. Voulgaris (New York);
Maria Vincenza Aloisi (Paris); Ann Natanson
(Rome). Valuable assistance was also provided by
Carolyn T. Chubet, Miriam Hsia (New York).

The Author: BARRIE PITT is the author of two books on naval history, and also wrote 1918—The Last Act, an account of the final year of World War I. He was the editor of the eight-volume Histories of the First and Second World Wars published in Great Britain, and the editor-in-chief of a paperback series, Ballantine's Illustrated History of World War II.

The Consultants: COL. JOHN R. ELTING, USA (Ret.), is a military historian, author of The Battle of Bunker's Hill, A Military History and Atlas of the Napoleonic Wars. He edited Military Uniforms in North America: The Revolutionary Era and was associate editor of The West Point Atlas of American Wars.

HENRY H. ADAMS is a retired Navy captain who served aboard the destroyer U.S.S. Owen in the major campaigns of the Central Pacific during World War II. A native of Ann Arbor, Michigan, he was graduated from the University of Michigan, and received his M.A. and Ph.D. degrees from Columbia University. After his service in World War II he was a professor at the U.S. Naval Academy in Annapolis, Maryland, and was later head of the English Department at Illinois State University. His books include 1942: The Year That Doomed the Axis, Years of Deadly Peril, Years of Expectation, Years to Victory and Harry Hopkins: A Biography.

HANS-ADOLF JACOBSEN, Director of the Seminar for Political Science at the University of Bonn, is the co-author of Anatomy of the S.S., and editor of Decisive Battles of World War II: The German View.

DONALD MACINTYRE served with the Royal Navy during World War II as a commander of destroyers and convoy escort groups in the North Atlantic. He was awarded the Distinguished Service Order three times, the Distinguished Service Cross and the American Legion of Merit. Since his retirement in 1954 he has written more than a score of books on naval historical subjects, including U-Boat Killer and Narvik.

CHAPTERS

PICTURE ESSAYS

CONTENTS

THE BATTLE'S FIRST VICTIMS

The British aircraft carrier Courageous, torpedoed off Ireland by a German U-boat, heels over before sinking on September 17, 1939, with a loss of 518 lives.

THE TORPEDOES TAKE THEIR TOLL

Regent Tiger: *November 21, 1939. Black smoke billows up from the burning British tanker as she starts to sink just after being torpedoed.*

The last months of 1939 were widely described as the time of the "phony war"; after Poland fell, there was little land fighting anywhere. But it was different at sea. There, the war raged with a fury that presaged a long, bloody conflict.

Not 10 hours after Prime Minister Neville Chamberlain's announcement that war had begun, a U-boat torpedoed the British liner *Athenia*. Of the 1,400 passengers aboard (many of whom were fleeing the war in Europe), 112 lost their lives, including 28 Americans.

In the weeks that followed, Hitler's sea wolves—as his submarine force was called—struck time and again at the merchant shipping so vital to Britain's economic survival. Even British warships fell prey to submarine sorties. The first big casualty was the aircraft carrier *Courageous* in September, followed within a month by the battleship *Royal Oak*.

The losses of matériel were appalling, but what happened to the crews and passengers stunned all who heard of their fate. In the frightful minutes between a torpedo's hull-rending crash and the stricken vessel's death plunge, those who were not killed outright by the explosion often were crushed by collapsing steel, scalded to death by steam from ruptured boilers, or drowned by the inrushing sea. When there was fire, survivors often faced another kind of torture, struggling in water whose surface was aflame with oil.

While the torpedoes wreaked massive destruction, magnetic mines—laid in large numbers along coastal waterways by submarines, surface ships and the Luftwaffe—took a terrible toll of their own. At the same time, in more distant waters, powerful raiders like the pocket battleship *Graf Spee* were blasting victims out of the sea.

By the end of 1939, the box score on the Battle of the Atlantic had mounted frighteningly. Within the short space of four months, U-boats, mines, airplanes and surface raiders had sent more than 215 merchant ships—a staggering 748,000 tons of shipping—to the bottom, along with two of Britain's largest warships. More than 1,500 lives had been lost—and it was clear that despite the lull on land, a long war lay ahead on the world's waters.

Athenia: *September 3, 1939. A U-boat casualty off Scotland on the first day of the War, the doomed British liner begins to settle by the stern.*

Gipsy: November 22, 1939. *The British destroyer sinks off the English coast after hitting a mine while going to the rescue of three downed Nazi airmen.*

Doric Star: December 2, 1939. *The 10,086-ton British freighter explodes amidships after being fired upon by the German raider Graf Spee.*

San Galisto: December 2, 1939. *Escape ladders dangle from the deck of the British tanker as she sinks off the English coast, the victim of two mines.*

Aragonite: November 22, 1939. *With only her funnel and masts above water, the British minesweeper becomes another mine fatality off England.*

Royal Oak: October 14, 1939. *The World War I battleship, seen in a prouder moment, became a U-boat victim at Scapa Flow with the loss of 833 aboard.*

1

Shortly after 7 o'clock on the evening of October 13, 1939, off the Orkney Islands, the waters of the North Sea parted above the rising conning tower of the German submarine *U-47*, and a few seconds later the hatch was thrown back. Lieut. Commander Günther Prien, one of the most promising of Hitler's U-boat commanders, tense after a day spent on the bottom, pulled himself up onto the bridge. As he did so, he suppressed an oath.

Nature had played an infuriating trick. Although weather conditions were perfect, as had been predicted—a moonless night, choppy but not boisterous seas and a fresh breeze—all was apparently ruined by that spectacular freak of arctic lighting, the aurora borealis. Billows of colorful light streamed across the northern skies, illuminating one half of the horizon and threatening to betray the presence of the submarine.

Briefly, Prien considered abandoning his mission. But weeks would pass before ideal conditions of tide and moon would prevail again. Moreover, the high morale that had crackled through the *U-47* since he had briefed his men on their mission might be impossible to recapture.

For the 31-year-old Prien, the *U-47* was his first command and this was his first big assignment. He had been chosen by Commodore Karl Dönitz, head of the German submarine arm, to carry out the first special U-boat operation of the War: an audacious attack on the British fleet right in the middle of its home base at Scapa Flow.

In all of World War II, no U-boat commander would be asked to perform a more daring or difficult mission. Scapa Flow, a deepwater, almost landlocked basin in the Orkney Islands, was one of the most heavily guarded anchorages in the world. Its entrances were blocked by sunken ships, mines and nets, and patrolled by the Royal Navy. Moreover, a submarine attempting to sneak in was likely to encounter exceptionally heavy currents.

Scapa Flow held a special, bitter significance for the Germans. The main units of the German fleet had been interned there after World War I. In 1919, while the Allies were arguing over the final disposition of the fleet, the skeleton German crews that were manning the ships scuttled and sank most of them.

Now the Germans were returning to Scapa Flow. Dönitz himself had planned the operation, studying aerial photo-

UNLEASHING THE SEA WOLVES

graphs to find the best route into the anchorage, and personally picking Prien to lead the attack (he reminded Prien, as he did so, that in World War I, two German submarines had attempted a similar attack on the British fleet in Scapa Flow, and had not returned).

On the morning of October 8, the *U-47* slipped from her mooring at Kiel in northern Germany and passed through the Kiel Canal into the North Sea. The crew members were still in the dark as to the nature of their mission, but suspicions that it was something special were aroused when the U-boat spotted a pall of smoke on the horizon and Prien ordered a dive without even investigating. Only when the submarine was lying on the surface not far from the Orkneys, recharging her batteries and renewing her supply of compressed air, did Prien break the news to his first watch officer, Engelbert Endrass. "Hold onto something, Endrass," he said. "We're going into Scapa Flow."

Prien then told the rest of the crew, and ordered up a special feast to mark the occasion. It was a strange celebration. The U-boat submerged, and the men sat down to a meal of pork ribs and cabbage. To reduce the risk of detection, the cook, as he served, padded about quietly with his feet wrapped in rags.

Seven and a half hours later, the *U-47*, now on the surface, slipped into Holm Sound, one of three entrances to Scapa Flow. Aerial photographs had indicated to Dönitz that the Kirk Sound entrance on the north of Holm Sound— a slender channel between islands, which was almost completely blocked by three sunken ships—might be negotiated by a daring navigator in a small craft. As midnight neared, Prien stood on his bridge peering into the channel, brightly lit by the flickering aurora. The land closed in on both sides, and the funnels and masts of the sunken ships loomed menacingly above the water ahead. "It is a very eerie sight," Prien recorded in his log. "On land everything is dark, high in the sky are the flickering northern lights, so that the bay, surrounded by high mountains, is directly lit up from above. The blockships lie in the sound, ghostly as the wings in a theater."

To the north, along the coast road of the island off to his right, Prien could see an Orkney Islander cycling homeward, his head lamp glowing weakly in the darkness. Prien had memorized the chart, and he did not bother to refer to

it as he guided the U-boat through the passage. He was safely past one of the sunken ships—a two-masted schooner lying in approximately 30 feet of water—when a sudden current turned the U-boat to starboard. The submarine fouled a cable of one of the sunken ships and Prien felt the hull touch bottom. Carefully, delicately, he disengaged the *U-47*, turned slightly to port and then with a difficult, rapid maneuver whisked his boat through the gap. By 12:30 on the morning of October 14, he was inside Scapa Flow.

There another jolting surprise awaited him. As the *U-47* prowled toward the main anchorage with her conning tower hatch open and decks slightly awash, Prien found himself surrounded by a wide expanse of empty water where he had expected to find the Home Fleet. With mounting impatience and anxiety, he edged northward. At last his persistence was rewarded. First he made out the low shapes of destroyers anchored close inshore; then, emerging from the outline of a hill behind them, the masts of two great ships rose against the sky. One was the battleship *Royal Oak* and the other the seaplane carrier *Pegasus* (Prien actually mistook her for the battle cruiser *Repulse*). The U-boat commander gazed with fascination at the *Royal Oak,* and then turned to Endrass. "Here, take a peep at that," he said. "There's another one behind her."

The *U-47* was now 4,000 yards from her quarry, in position for a sensational kill. The four bow torpedo tubes were aimed at the overlapping silhouettes of the two British ships, and Prien gave the firing order. A hiss of air pressure followed, the boat recoiled at the shock of discharge, and the slow, deliberate seconds ticked by as the torpedoes ran.

Three minutes later, with a solid thump, a solitary torpedo exploded harmlessly—evidently against either the *Royal Oak's* bow or her anchor chain. Puzzled and bitterly disappointed, Prien turned his craft away. As he did so he discharged his stern torpedo; it too was wide of the mark.

By now the *U-47's* situation was precarious; surely the whole British fleet was alerted. Prien's instinct was to run for safety. But as he waited apprehensively for the counterattack that must surely come, he began to realize that, astonishingly, no one on board any of the vessels anchored around him suspected his presence even yet. He had no way of knowing it, but both Captain W. G. Benn of the *Royal Oak* and the commander of the 2nd Battle Squadron,

Rear-Admiral H. E. C. Blagrove, who was also on board, had attributed the torpedo explosion to some undetermined internal cause.

Incredibly, Prien had been granted another chance by the British, and this time he proposed to make the most of it. While members of his crew labored to reload the torpedo tubes, he coolly circled for position under the still-flickering northern lights.

Again he gave the order to fire. Again the submariners waited tensely as the torpedoes sped toward their targets.

Suddenly everything happened at once. "There is a loud explosion, roar and rumbling," Prien noted in his log. "Then come columns of water, followed by columns of fire, and splinters fly through the air. The harbor springs to life. Destroyers are lit up, signalling starts on every side, and on land, 200 meters away from me, cars roar along the roads. A battleship has been sunk, a second damaged, and the other three torpedoes have gone to blazes."

Thirteen minutes after the attack, the battered hulk of the *Royal Oak* turned on her side and slid below the surface of Scapa Flow, taking with her 833 officers and men.

The submariners were exultant; but their worst ordeal lay ahead. As Prien turned the *U-47* and sped away toward the escape channel, a clearly visible wake of white water followed behind the U-boat. To port, the land came down close and an automobile speeding along the coast road braked to a halt as its headlights caught the *U-47*'s conning tower. Abruptly the car turned around and shot back the way it had come, leaving Prien certain that he had been located and would soon be attacked.

The tide was sluicing in from the east; even with diesels and electric motors both wide open, the *U-47* crept along at only slightly more than one knot, yet created a high, curling wave to either side. Astern, Scapa Flow was churning with activity, and one of the searching destroyers was drawing near, her searchlight probing ominously. Yard by yard, the *U-47* forced her way toward the narrow gap by which she had entered, at one point barely avoiding a collision with a wooden pier jutting from the island shore.

As the U-boat swung out into Holm Sound, the pursuing destroyer turned and dropped a pattern of depth charges well to the rear, her electronic submarine-tracking device probably having mistaken a sunken wreck for the *U-47*. It

was the last close brush. As the U-boat slipped triumphantly back into the North Sea, Prien made one more log note: "The glow from Scapa Flow is still visible. . . ."

For years the German Navy had been the stepchild of the Third Reich, neglected in favor of the Army, pet of ex-Corporal Hitler—and the Luftwaffe, darling of Hermann Göring. Repeatedly Dönitz had argued that the only weapon that could throttle Britain was a large submarine fleet; he had been ignored.

But the Scapa Flow exploit was an eye opener. Two days afterward, on October 16, Grand Admiral Erich Raeder, the commander in chief of the German Navy, distributed a memorandum. "The Führer grants permission for the following measures," it began. There followed a series of war orders; the important one read: "All merchant ships defi-

nitely recognized as enemy (British or French) can be torpedoed without warning."

The Raeder order marked the culmination of an increasingly tough German submarine policy. At the beginning of the War, U-boats were still conforming to the Hague Convention, which prohibited attacks without warning on enemy passenger and merchant ships. One British ship—the passenger liner *Athenia*—had been sunk without warning, but the U-boat commander had acted in direct violation of Hitler's orders.

As time passed and it became apparent to Hitler that there would be no quick end to the War, the restrictions against submarine warfare were relaxed. On September 23, the Führer decided that all merchant ships using radios should be halted and sunk or taken captive. The next day,

an order forbidding the sinking of French ships was rescinded. On September 30, restrictions against attacks in the North Sea were removed. Two days later, attacks against darkened ships off the coasts of France and Britain were approved, and two days after that the area in which unrestricted attacks were allowed was extended to 170 miles west of Ireland.

Raeder's order after Prien's exploit, removing all remaining restrictions on attacks against Allied merchant ships, turned the U-boats loose against the most important category of enemy ships. Passenger ships still were supposed to be warned. But by the middle of November, even that rule had been dropped.

Two weeks after the *U-47*'s visit to Scapa Flow, Günther Prien and his crew were the guests of their Führer at the Chancellery in Berlin; there Prien was decorated with the coveted *Ritterkreuz*, or Knight's Cross to the Iron Cross.

In the coming months the intensified submarine warfare was to have the gravest consequences for the hard-pressed British. Control of the seas was absolutely essential to Britain. To prosecute its war effort—even to feed its population—the island nation had to import food and raw materials from North and South America and the farthest reaches of its empire in Asia and the Pacific. Mutton and butter from New Zealand, wool from Australia, beef from Argentina, lumber from Canada—all had to come in by freighter. Iron ore was brought in from Africa, rubber from Malaya and grain from Canada, the United States and Argentina. Oil, critical to the running of Britain's war machine, had to be imported over thousands of miles of open sea from the Middle East, the United States, and the Dutch West Indies in highly vulnerable tankers.

To wage any sort of war would prove impossible without an uninterrupted flow into British ports of nearly a million tons of essential materials every week. A fleet of 3,000 merchant ships was required to transport these critical supplies, and almost any day 2,500 of these vessels were at sea. Furthermore, troop reinforcements would be flowing into Britain from across the seas. Both the Canadian and Australian governments were anxious to send men to serve in the European war. As World War II progressed, more and more troops from other parts of the Empire—from South Africa and Rhodesia, New Zealand and India—would be arriving

The daring raid by German submarine U-47 on the British Home Fleet's base at Scapa Flow—located in Scotland's Orkney Islands (inset map at left)—began (red line, large map) when the U-boat entered the protected anchorage of Kirk Sound, and spotted the battleship Royal Oak and the carrier Pegasus. The U-47 scored one inconclusive hit on the Royal Oak, and turned to escape. When no alarm was raised, the submarine circled, and this time sank the battleship. She escaped (gray line) through Kirk Sound. Back in Germany, the U-boat's skipper, Günther Prien (above, right), received a hero's welcome from Commodore Dönitz at the Kriegsmarine base in Wilhelmshaven and was awarded the Knight's Cross. Dönitz was promoted to rear admiral for conceiving the attack.

to play the same role their fathers had played 25 years earlier against the same enemy. Perhaps even the Americans might come in again. All of this meant that steadily growing numbers of ships had to be protected.

The Germans knew, of course, that seaborne commerce was vital to Britain's survival. The admirals of the German Navy had made plans to use battleships and cruisers to sink merchant ships on the high seas. They also planned to sow the waters around Britain with deadly mines, and to em-

ploy armed merchantmen disguised to look like innocent freighters to sneak up on unwary captains and blow their ships out of the water. But Dönitz and his staff had always known that their chief hope of blockading Britain lay in the U-boats, which could sink the ships that were bringing supplies and troops across the Atlantic.

In the months that followed, the German subs missed no opportunity. The British, on their part, fought back desperately. They attacked the German surface ships by air and sea, they waged unrelenting warfare against the submarines, and they established their own blockade of the German-occupied European continent. The resulting Battle of the Atlantic was one of the fiercest—and in many ways the most crucial—of all the armed confrontations of World War II. So deadly was it, and so close did the German submarines come to severing Britain's lifeline, that Winston Churchill, Prime Minister through all but a few months of the War, would later recall: "The only thing that ever really frightened me during the war was the U-boat peril."

The Battle of the Atlantic was one that the British at the outset were ill-equipped to fight, even though Britain was the world's foremost sea power.

Britain's unpreparedness stemmed from a variety of misjudgments. First there was the widely held view that the Germans would never again resort to the kind of merciless, unrestricted submarine warfare that had been waged in World War I. There were good reasons for this belief. The London Submarine Protocol of 1936, which the Germans had signed, expressly outlawed the sinking of any unescorted merchant ship without warning. The Protocol also forbade the sinking of any ship without first searching it and discovering contraband aboard. Moreover, the crew of any merchant ship that was attacked had to be assured a safe means of reaching shore, their own lifeboats being deemed insufficient unless land was near. This meant that U-boats would have to surface and expose themselves before making an attack, becoming vulnerable to any ship carrying even light armament and to whatever reinforcements the victim's radio communications could summon.

It was naïve to expect warring nations to honor such legal limitations. In fact, the German Navy's battle instructions contained the following, not unreasonable, order: "Fighting methods will never fail to be employed merely be-

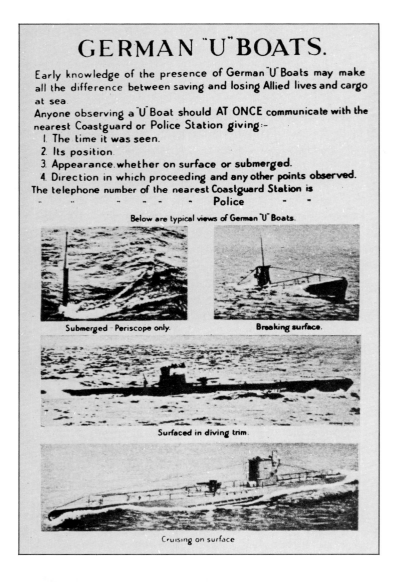

A poster from a shop in the Orkney Islands exhorts the inhabitants to watch for enemy submarines. Featuring four views of U-boats, the poster lists the facts to be noted and reported to the nearest authorities. In the early months of the War, the Admiralty circulated thousands of these posters for display in public places in the coastal areas of Britain.

cause some international regulations are opposed to them."

Apart from the misplaced faith in treaty obligations and world opinion, there were other reasons within the Admiralty for Britain's lack of preparation for all-out U-boat warfare. The old-line admirals who ran the Navy had been more concerned with Germany's emerging surface fleet than with the potential submarine menace. They envisaged the probability of classic battleship confrontations in which huge battlewagons would try to pound each other into submission, as had occurred during the great World War I Battle of Jutland.

Britain's naval building program in the late 1930s was tailored to that kind of warfare. The five new battleships, six aircraft carriers and 19 heavy cruisers ordered between 1936 and 1939 were better suited for fighting surface fleets than for escorting merchant ships or hunting and killing U-boats.

But as the War got under way, the Admiralty believed that the combined British and French navies were sufficient

New U-boats get final fittings at the Germania Shipyard in Kiel. Krupp, Germany's biggest armament and munitions maker, launched the U-1, the first post-World War I submarine, in secrecy from this yard in 1935. By 1942, the Krupp shipyard was building 20 submarines a year; by the end of the War, it had built 168 of Germany's 1,099 U-boats.

to handle almost any contingency. Although the French Navy was operating chiefly in the western Mediterranean, in the closing months of 1939 it still had units in the Channel ports and the Bay of Biscay. U-boats scored notable successes against shipping during this period, and U-boat strength and efficiency could be expected to grow in the coming months. But so would the antisubmarine potential of the British and the French, and it did not appear to be beyond the capacity of the Allies to contain the threat. As the Admiralty viewed the situation, there was cause to watch the U-boats closely and to develop efficient countermeasures as rapidly as possible, but there was no necessity for undue alarm.

There was still another reason why the Admiralty did not take the submarine threat more seriously; it stemmed from an undue reliance on a weapon developed between the wars. This device led the British to the false conclusion that even if the Germans did resort to all-out U-boat warfare, Allied shipping would be adequately protected.

Toward the end of World War I, a body had been established called the Allied Submarine Detection Investigation Committee. The Committee had produced a range-finding device which, under ideal circumstances, could not only detect a submerged submarine but could also reveal its position. The device, called asdic, from the initials of the Committee (the American version was called sonar), consisted of a transmitter-receiver encased in a metal dome fitted under the hull of the carrying vessel. The transmitter could send out sound impulses on any selected bearing; the receiver would then pick up the impulses when they struck an object and were reflected. The asdic "ping" was a sound that would become familiar to tens of thousands of seamen during the War years, frighteningly so to submariners, who could also hear it. An experienced operator could tell from the pitch of the asdic echo whether a submarine was approaching or moving away. Musicians, with their keen sense of pitch, were particularly good at making this distinction and were much sought after as asdic operators.

The transmitter-receiver was designed so that it could be trained around like a searchlight. When connected to a compass, it would give the direction in which the submarine lay. The time between transmission of the impulse and the return of its echo revealed the range.

As the system was improved and perfected during the War, a group of ships with overlapping asdics could search a wide expanse of the sea, locating all lurking U-boats in the area. But at the beginning of the War, there were serious limitations to asdic's usefulness. The vast majority of the asdic operators were men who had been called up from civilian life and given only a three-month training course before being sent out to sea. Until they acquired extensive experience with the equipment, all echoes were the same: rocks, sunken wrecks, schools of fish, U-boats, even differences in temperature between layers of water. And the number of depth charges carried by any one vessel was not so great that they could be scattered around the ocean every time an ex-civilian who had just finished a training course thought he had located a U-boat.

Even for experienced operators, there were serious technical problems. The sound beam sent out by asdic was conical in shape. The cone pointed away from the transmitting ship, which meant that the area covered by the asdic beams widened with the distance. Within the range of asdic—about 1,500 yards—the farther away a submarine was from the hunter ship, the more likely it was to be spotted. As the submarine and the hunter came closer to each other, the beam narrowed until contact with the sub was lost. U-boat commanders, listening to the ping, quickly

became adept at taking advantage of this gap in contact. The Admiralty was confident, however, that this problem could be overcome, given more time and sufficient training.

But there was another, more serious limitation to asdic. The listening device could be used underwater only. It could not locate submarines on the surface. Aware of the shortcomings of asdic, the canny chief of the German submarine arm, Karl Dönitz, simply ordered his boats to attack at night and from the surface. For the rest of the War, submarines—despite their name—operated for the most part above water, and after dark. They were not only less visible and less audible that way; at top speed, they could travel at 17 to 18 knots on the surface compared with seven to eight knots when submerged. The submarines usually submerged only when danger threatened or a rare daylight attack was to be launched.

The Admiralty was not totally blind to the U-boat threat, of course. The need for escorts to protect merchant convoys had been recognized. Moreover, the urgent necessity for building more antisubmarine vessels was brought home forcefully in April 1939, when Hitler announced his intention to exceed the limits of the 1935 Anglo-German treaty, which stipulated that the two nations would have submarine fleets of the same tonnage.

In response, the Admiralty immediately ordered 56 new escort vessels, the first of the Flower-class corvettes, small, highly maneuverable craft that could be produced quickly and inexpensively in Britain's shipyards.

But the first of these ships would not be ready until the spring of 1940, and it would be a long time after that before there would be enough escort vessels to go around.

When there were, it was preordained by Admiralty policy that they would be improperly used. For British naval planners were ignoring a critical and hard-learned lesson of World War I. In 1917 the Allies had found that the answer to the submarine menace was the convoy. By organizing merchant ships into groups and escorting them with warships, the British had cut their shipping losses by 80 per cent. But in the first year of World War II, a large proportion of the available escort vessels were uselessly employed on search and patrol missions in the ocean's empty spaces. This was wasteful of ships and fuel, and it provided no protection for ships that were traveling at a distance from the patrols. In the early weeks of the War, therefore, many ships were left to travel without escort, and shipping losses were heavy. In the month of September, even before Hitler approved unrestricted submarine attacks, the *Athenia*, the aircraft carrier *Courageous* and 41 merchantmen were sunk.

Eventually, the Admiralty moved to establish an effective convoy system. But it was not until 1943 that Allied ships in the North Atlantic finally got the protection they needed. By that time the battle had been very nearly lost.

At the outset of the War, however, the Germans were not at all sure of their prospects on the Atlantic—despite the high toll of Allied ships (roughly 1.3 per day) during the War's first month. Germany had only 56 U-boats, and 10 of them were not operational at the outbreak of the War. Of the 46 operational submarines, moreover, 24 were small boats most suitable for training and coastal operations—primarily mine laying. And of the 22 oceangoing craft of 500 tons and above, only about a third could be hunting enemy ships at any one time. Experience had established that approximately one third of any submarine force would always be in port for rest, refitting and replenishing while another third would be en route to or from the hunting grounds.

There was an additional problem for the German subs. The long haul from the bases at Hamburg, Wilhelmshaven and Kiel through the North Sea and over the top of the Orkney Islands meant that the time actually spent on patrol in the Atlantic would be greatly shortened. In fact, during the early months of the War, only a handful of German U-boats were operating in the Atlantic at any one time.

When the War broke out in 1939, Raeder, keenly aware of the problems confronting the German Navy, was extremely apprehensive. A veteran of the Battle of Jutland and since 1928 the Navy's highest-ranking officer, he had kept a close eye on the British Navy, and he believed that the German fleet was "in no way very adequately equipped for the great struggle with Great Britain."

Dönitz was equally aware of the weakness of the German Navy, and had been pressing for more submarines. Raeder's chief subordinate, he was a former World War I U-boat commander whose energy and determination were not easily suppressed. Near the end of the earlier war, Dönitz' submarine had been sunk in the Mediterranean. He had

A German contact mine, live with high explosive, rests menacingly on a Dutch North Sea beach in the fall of 1939, after having ripped away from its anchor. Usually submerged in coastal waters, such mines were detonated when a ship bent or broke one of the protruding spikes. Their use by Germany violated an international treaty outlawing them.

been captured and had spent almost 10 months in a British prison camp, and imprisonment had given him an opportunity for contemplation—about submarine warfare in general and offensive tactics in particular.

Following his repatriation, Dönitz remained in the service as one of the 15,000 naval personnel that Germany was allowed under the Versailles Treaty. Because the Treaty limited the German Navy to surface ships, Dönitz was unable to resume his U-boat career. Submarines were seldom far from his mind, however, and while serving with the surface fleet he demonstrated a gift for leadership—an incisive directness coupled with a warmth and sense of personal concern for his men—that was to stand him in good stead later on. In due course he was promoted to command of the modern light cruiser *Emden*. He had just returned to Wilhelmshaven from fleet exercises in July 1935, when Admiral Raeder came aboard his ship with important news. The Anglo-German treaty providing for U-boat parity had been signed. Germany was to have a submarine force again and Dönitz was to command it. The years of training and planning were not to be wasted after all.

Dönitz set about with enthusiasm to rebuild Germany's submarine fleet, and in spite of the years of neglect, he knew that the U-boats and the cadres to run them were readily available to him. Since 1922, German civilians had been quietly designing new submarines for a Dutch firm in The Hague, which was in fact a front for certain German shipyards. Germany's own shipyards had also been secretly busy. Ten days after the 1935 pact became effective, the *U-1*, the first new German submarine, was launched from a heavily guarded shed in the shipyard at Kiel. By the start of the next year, Dönitz had a flotilla of 12 small U-boats.

The new boats were considerably more sophisticated and more menacing than their World War I predecessors. Stronger batteries enabled them to stay underwater for longer periods of time. Their electrically-powered torpedoes—when perfected—left no telltale wakes and were equipped with magnetic firing devices designed to explode under a ship's keel with maximum effect.

To achieve the full impact of his U-boats, Dönitz envisioned a "tonnage war," an all-out campaign designed to sink the maximum enemy tonnage per submarine per day. He believed that the North Atlantic would be the decisive theater of operations and foresaw that when war came—especially if it was against the British—the U-boats would have to carry out their attacks against convoys of merchantmen guarded by naval escorts. A single U-boat in such circumstances might inflict some damage, but a concentration of U-boats, a "wolf pack" as it was to be called, would wreak far greater havoc. There were two problems: to locate the convoys, and to concentrate the U-boats.

The problem of concentration had been made much easier during the interwar years by the improvement in radio communications. Now U-boats on the surface could not only talk to one another; they could communicate with headquarters hundreds of miles away.

A more difficult problem was that of locating the convoys. The most effective method was to spread a picket line of U-boats across the main shipping routes and the approaches to the enemy ports. The first U-boat to sight a convoy could report to headquarters, which would then concentrate submarines for an attack.

This strategy, of course, would require large numbers of U-boats. Dönitz believed that 100 U-boats could do more damage than all the battle cruisers ever built. Given 300 subs, he was confident he could sever England's lifelines.

But Dönitz had to fight for his ideas at every turn. The Navy ran a poor third to the Army and the Luftwaffe in terms of money, matériel and men. Even when Raeder managed to impress Hitler with the Navy's potential, top priority was likely to be given to surface vessels—especially the battleships and pocket battleships, which the Führer thought looked so splendid and which attracted so much attention whenever any of them ventured abroad.

In 1938 a sudden shift in strategy forced the German military services to re-evaluate their roles. Up to that point, planning had been predicated upon a conflict with Poland or France. Now Hitler instructed his military chiefs to add Great Britain to the roster of possible future opponents. The Navy, recognizing its unreadiness for such a war, began a major reappraisal of its overall strategy and its priorities for warship construction.

After months of intense intraservice debate, Raeder presented two alternative plans to Hitler. The less expensive and more quickly achievable plan emphasized tonnage war against British shipping by Dönitz' submarines as well as armed merchantmen and pocket battleships. The other—known as the Z Plan—included submarines only as one part of a balanced force of new aircraft carriers, battleships, cruisers and destroyers that could challenge Great Britain's control of the sea.

To the dismay of Dönitz, Hitler opted for the balanced fleet and in January 1939 ordered that top priority be given to its construction. But within nine months, Germany was at war, and the plan became one of the first casualties.

When the Second World War broke out, Dönitz had every available U-boat—46 in all—ready for action in the Atlantic, the North Sea and the Baltic. But he could not keep even a limited number of submarines at sea on a sustained basis, and for a year it was all he could do to replace his U-boats as fast as they were being sunk—a rate of about two submarines per month.

Both the Germans and the British supplemented their battle fleets with another deadly weapon: they sowed their own coasts and the enemy's with thousands of mines, lethal floating explosives that could block ports, tie up convoys and blow up ships. The British, conforming to international agreement, employed only the conventional contact mine, which was moored underwater by cable, and exploded when struck by a ship's hull. The Germans had fewer mines, but some of them were of a more deadly magnetic variety. Planted on the seabed in shallow water, they were set off by the mere proximity of a ship's steel hull.

The British did not find out how to deal with these mines until the summer of 1940, after they had recovered a German mine dropped inadvertently by the Luftwaffe on the mudflats of the Thames estuary. Until then, the magnetic mines defied sweeping, and in November and December of 1939 they sank more ships than Dönitz' submarines.

In the following months, shipping losses—from mines and other causes—mounted rapidly. By the spring of 1940, Britain and its suppliers had lost some 460 merchant ships within a few brief months of warfare. Nevertheless, shipping losses still seemed to be within acceptable limits. Germany's smaller surface fleet appeared incapable of any massive challenge to the Royal Navy. Moreover, an unexpected lull occurred in the U-boat warfare, as Hitler sent his subs to Norway to support the invasion of that country.

But the march of events on land soon radically altered the tempo of the Battle of the Atlantic. On May 10, 1940, the German armies began their great sweep across the Low Countries and Northern France. Holland fell within five days, Belgium in 18 days, and by June 4 most of the British Army had been forced to withdraw from the Continent at Dunkirk. Norway fell on June 8, and by June 17 France was suing for peace.

The British took over six French warships, and destroyed a substantial part of the French fleet at Mers-el-Kebir in Algeria (the bulk of the remaining ships were scuttled by the French themselves at Toulon in 1942). In the meantime, German troops arrived at the Channel ports and on the coast of the Bay of Biscay, and German U-boat crews were soon relaxing in the cafés of Lorient and Nantes. Senior German naval officers—the recently promoted Admiral Dönitz among them—examined the port facilities at Brest and Saint-Nazaire and were soon gazing speculatively out across the bay toward the wide reaches of the Atlantic.

To the British Admiralty, it was clear that the Royal Navy must be prepared to face a new threat: U-boats operating out of the nearby Biscay ports and from Norwegian bases at Bergen and Trondheim. From these bases, U-boats could operate in the Atlantic for greatly lengthened periods of time, receiving more effective guidance and support from squadrons of long-range, land-based planes operating out of Occupied France and Norway. Moreover, the greatly improved situation for the submarines meant that Germany would surely accelerate its U-boat building program.

All of this was happening at a critical time for the Royal Navy. The loss of the French Navy had greatly reduced the number of ships available to combat the U-boats, and had enormously expanded the areas to be covered by the Royal Navy. Moreover, Italy's entry into the conflict in June 1940, plus the need to take over total responsibility for the Mediterranean, imposed an even greater strain.

By now, German surface raiders were presenting a growing threat to Allied shipping. U-boats in increasing numbers were intensifying their efforts with deadly new tactics. The Battle of the Atlantic was beginning its steep climb to a crescendo of violence and destruction that would come close to severing the lifeline to Britain.

ZANY SAGA OF THE ZAMZAM

Ignoring the perils of war at sea, a uniformed ambulance driver and a pith-helmeted Ping-Pong player join other passengers for a stroll early in the voyage.

A PHANTOM RAIDER'S UNLIKELY TARGET

In April 1941 the rickety Egyptian liner *Zamzam* steamed down through the South Atlantic, bound from New York to South Africa and Egypt with a motley complement of European refugees, American missionary families, young volunteer ambulance drivers, North Carolina tobaccomen and French-Canadian priests. It was eight months before America's entry into the War, and the 138 Americans and 202 other passengers were about to become unwitting participants—and pawns—in the Battle of the Atlantic.

Five days out of Recife, Brazil, her last port of call before Cape Town, the *Zamzam*'s British captain picked up the distress call of a Norwegian ship being chased by a German raider. Alarmed, the *Zamzam* changed her course abruptly, veering sharply to the south. But next morning the horizon was empty, and the ship resumed her leisurely passage toward Cape Town.

Shortly after midnight on April 16, the *Zamzam* steamed into the path of the notorious German raider *Atlantis*, which was traveling disguised as the Norwegian cargo ship *Tamesis*. The *Zamzam* was completely blacked out, a procedure that was not normally followed by ships of neutral nations. Moreover, her profile was identical to that of sister ships that had served as troop carriers for Great Britain in World War I and had subsequently been converted into Royal Navy Auxiliary cruisers.

Mistaking the liner for one of these warships, the *Atlantis* stalked her and, just before dawn, struck. Mortally wounded by shelling, the *Zamzam* began sinking as bewildered passengers and panicking Egyptian crewmen abandoned her. After being picked up by the raider, the Zamzammers were transferred to the German freighter *Dresden* for a wild, zigzagging 33-day ride into the North Atlantic. Among the passengers were LIFE photographer David E. Scherman and FORTUNE editor Charles J. V. Murphy, who had boarded the *Zamzam* at Recife on their way to assignments in Africa. With his camera, Scherman made a record of the passengers' strange odyssey, from the moment he boarded the *Zamzam* to disembarkation in Occupied France.

Banner headlines announce the disappearance of the Zamzam in 1941. The map below traces the journey of the liner's "missing" passengers—from New York to South America and on to the spot in the South Atlantic where they were transferred from the sinking ship to the raider and then to a German freighter, which circled indecisively for eight days before finally heading north. The freighter veered a bit, on hearing that a British convoy was nearby, then turned east for Saint-Jean-de-Luz in Occupied France.

New York World-Telegram

CLOSING WALL ST. PRICES
Real Estate, Page 26

PRICE THREE CENTS

VOL. 73.—NO. 272—IN TWO SECTIONS—SECTION ONE   NEW YORK, MONDAY, MAY 19, 1941.

196 AMERICANS FEARED LOST WITH EGYPTIAN MERCY SHIP

| Agreement Ends Hard Coal Stoppage | Rail Unions Ask 30 P. C. Pay Boost | Roosevelt Due To State Policy, Barkley Hints | Passengers Aboard Ship Reported Lost | **Zamzam Missing a Month; 'Enemy Action' Blamed** |

Posing as the Tamesis, the notorious raider Atlantis was photographed by LIFE's David Scherman from a lifeboat just after she attacked the Zamzam.

The pretty wife of a Royal Air Force pilot stationed in Egypt whiles away a tropical afternoon in conversation at the ship's rail with a British businessman.

A LANGUOROUS SHIPBOARD LIFE

The passengers aboard the *Zamzam* were a mixed lot, and in the days before the raider struck, each group had to find its own solution for passing the time. Stern and righteous, the missionaries organized sunrise and evening services and spent the long days at sea studying Swahili or arguing over the Gospel.

Determined to have a good time, the two dozen young ambulance drivers, en route to Africa to help Free French forces fighting there, laid siege to the small bar aft. They played pranks on the disapproving missionaries and flirted with the ship's nurses and the RAF wives who were on their way to their husbands in Egypt.

Both the high-living ambulance drivers and the sober missionaries were scorned by the six hard-drinking North Carolina tobaccomen, who were traveling to Africa to buy highly prized Rhodesian tobacco.

Looking over his passengers with a bemused eye, Captain William Gray Smith said that it was "bad luck to have so many Bible punchers and sky pilots aboard." As it turned out, bad luck was just ahead.

The *Zamzam's* bar offered customers a wide variety of alcoholic drinks, including one concoction named after the ship herself.

The adventure-hungry ambulance drivers chafed at shipboard tedium and kept the bar open late each night. The attack caught some of them hung over.

ABANDONING SHIP UNDER FIRE

The attack on the *Zamzam* came without warning. A passenger at the rail watched the *Atlantis* approach and suspected nothing. Elevating a half-dozen 5.9-inch guns and a 75mm cannon, the *Atlantis* fired at the *Zamzam*. One salvo hit amidships below the waterline.

Ignoring frantic signals of surrender, the raider pounded the *Zamzam* for 10 minutes. One round maimed Frank Vicovari, coleader of the ambulance drivers, and Dr. Robert Starling, a middle-aged British chiropractor. Another hurled a steel splinter into the brain of "Uncle Ned" Laughinghouse, dean of the tobaccomen.

The crippled *Zamzam* heeled to port but managed to stay afloat. Overloaded and shell-damaged lifeboats spilled passengers into the warm sea. Survivors paddled over to the raider and scrambled up a rope ladder. Still aboard the *Zamzam*, several of the ambulance drivers lingered in the bar. On the stern, a missionary nicknamed "Gabriel" refused to abandon ship, screaming that the sins of his shipmates had brought down the wrath of God. The raiders carried him away. Soon everyone was on the *Atlantis*, and the Germans faced an explosive diplomatic problem.

The battered Zamzam lists heavily to port 10 minutes after the predawn attack as crowded lifeboats head for the safety of the raider. Scherman, who took

FORTUNE editor Charles Murphy yells at the crew of the stricken Zamzam to hold a lifeboat for an injured RAF wife and a dachshund named Willy.

this and other photos, hid the film in Murphy's pockets before the Germans could confiscate it. Murphy covered the film with hands bandaged for rope burns.

THE ENEMY AS GRACIOUS HOST

Bernhard Rogge, the captain of the *Atlantis,* was dismayed by his catch. At sea since July 1939, sinking scores of Allied ships, he had picked up many survivors, but never a large group of American civilians. A tall, thoughtful, elegant man, he dreaded the international incident that could be made out of the attack on the *Zamzam.*

Rogge consulted Berlin as to how he might turn this setback into an advantage. He had his crew transfer the passengers' luggage, including the missionaries' water-logged Bibles, which were spread out on deck to dry. His sailors fed the children chocolate and took the wounded below for surgery. Rogge told a delegation headed by Captain Smith and editor Murphy that the *Zamzam,* as a ship of a noncombatant nation, should have had her lights on. (It emerged later that Captain Smith had been ordered by the British Admiralty to sail the *Zamzam* without lights, a circumstance that baffled the Germans, and was darkly construed by some authorities as part of a plot to precipitate an incident that would bring America into the War.)

Rogge promised he would transfer the Zamzammers to a neutral ship or put them ashore in a neutral nation. Then—as the captives watched helplessly—he had demolition crews scuttle the *Zamzam.* After that, there was no turning back.

Wounded in the attack, passengers rest in the hospital bay after surgery aboard the raider.

Passengers from the Zamzam watch the sinking of their ship from the deck of the Atlantis. Charges were set off by time fuses; in this sequence, recorded

Awaiting instructions on the raider's deck, ambulance drivers put up a jaunty front. Around them is the passengers' luggage, brought aboard by the German crew.

by Scherman, the liner sinks slowly from sight. A German officer told the photographer precisely where he should stand in order to get the best pictures.

Photographer Scherman (seated) plays the ocarina with the missionaries' pickup band on the Dresden.

MAKING THE MOST OF A PUZZLING JOURNEY

After a fitful night aboard the *Atlantis*, the Zamzammers awoke to discover that they had made a rendezvous with the freighter *Dresden*, the nearest German vessel at hand. Captain Rogge had to clear the *Atlantis* of captives but, as part of a clever plot that he had worked out with Berlin by radio, the Zamzammers were about to be kept at sea for more than a month. The *Dresden* would serve as their makeshift prison ship.

The women and children were jammed into the *Dresden*'s tiny passenger cabins, the men forced to make the best of sleeping in holds and whiling away the days on deck. Uncertain of their fate, and some of them sick with worry, they dreaded what would become of them next. They hoped to encounter a British warship, but feared submarines. And the meandering course of the *Dresden* revealed nothing. Each day the sun rose from a different quarter, indicating that course was being changed constantly without apparent purpose.

Frustrated, the Zamzammers constructed benches, a table, a latrine and showers—anything to keep busy and to make life more comfortable. Breakfast, eaten on deck, was a thin gruel they called "billboard paste"; supper was an unappetizing soup they christened "glop." But life had its comforts: the *Dresden* was equipped with a small pool for peacetime passengers, and the Zamzammers swam every day until they reached the chilly latitudes of the North Atlantic. Even then, dressed warmly, they played chess and backgammon on deck, and some speculated over possible destinations. Using an improvised sextant, and comparing their watches with the changing ship's time, they calculated their position daily but were no wiser as to where they were headed.

Nerves were fraying when the *Dresden* finally turned east, ran through the British blockade off the Bay of Biscay and headed for Occupied France.

Sharing tea and a meager lunch, husbands and wives bundle up against the cold wind off Labrador.

One of the ambulance drivers paints on a bulkhead the newly adopted nickname of the meandering Zamzammers, the "Wandering and Wondering Society."

Calisthenics keep the Zamzammers occupied on the Dresden but enthusiasm quickly waned.

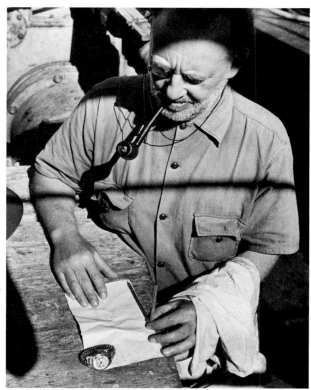

A British scholar works out the daily position of the freighter.

Landfall in France was a welcome sight, but the passengers were amused when a German pilot ran the Dresden aground briefly before reaching the shore.

A TARDY ARRIVAL IN OCCUPIED FRANCE

On May 21, 30 days after the *Zamzam* had been scheduled to arrive in Cape Town, the *Dresden* steamed into Saint-Jean-de-Luz, France. The timing was vital: the previous day the British Admiralty had announced that the *Zamzam* was a month overdue and presumed sunk. Another incident like the World War I sinking of the *Lusitania* seemed to be in the making.

Then Berlin coolly announced that, far from being harmed, the Americans were all alive and well in a French resort close to Biarritz, awaiting repatriation. Evidently, Berlin had kept the Zamzammers at sea so that it could top the news of the sinking. The *Zamzam* had been sunk, claimed Berlin, because she carried "contraband"—steel rails for the North African front.

After interrogation, the Americans were freed. Some Europeans were interned; the rest were repatriated.

The Germans took most of Scherman's films to censor in Berlin, but he managed to hide four rolls in a tube of toothpaste, a tube of shaving cream and two boxes of surgical gauze that were carried for him in a missionary doctor's bag until their train reached neutral Portugal.

Murphy and Scherman flew from Lisbon to New York, where LIFE published the photographs, among them Scherman's surreptitious picture of the *Atlantis* (page 27). Displayed in the wardroom of every British warship, this photograph enabled the cruiser H.M.S. *Devonshire* to identify the raider six months later, despite her *Tamesis* disguise, and sink her. In December, only days before America entered the War, Berlin inexplicably released the rest of Scherman's 1,500 photographs, and LIFE published the whole saga of the *Zamzam*.

A final touch was added to the mystery of the *Zamzam* one year later when Scherman photographed Anthony Eden on an assignment for LIFE. The British statesman remarked cryptically over tea: "You chaps on the *Zamzam* were quite a disappointment to us. We expected that incident to bring America into the War."

The Dresden's bearded carpenter says goodbye to one of his many new friends from the Zamzam.

2

"The surface forces can do no more than show that they know how to die gallantly."

So wrote the commander in chief of the German Navy, Grand Admiral Erich Raeder, on September 3, 1939, when both Great Britain and France, with their large navies, reacted to Hitler's invasion of Poland by declaring war on Germany. The admiral's gloomy foreboding reflected the critical unpreparedness of the German Navy.

For Raeder and his forces, the Second World War had come several years too soon. He had accepted the Führer's repeated assurances that the Navy would not have to be ready for combat duty until 1944 or 1945. At the beginning of the War, there were far too few operational U-boats in the Atlantic to pose a mortal threat to Allied shipping, and Germany's surface fleet was not numerically large enough to risk direct confrontations with the Royal Navy. The long-range construction program embodied in the ambitious *Z Plan*, a program that might eventually have enabled the German Navy to challenge Great Britain as a world sea power, had not been launched until January of 1939. As a result, Germany's ships would have to depend on stealth, power and speed in the months to come. And it was clear that these qualities alone might not be sufficient.

Germany's surface navy in 1939 consisted of two small battleships, three "pocket battleships," eight cruisers, and 34 destroyers and torpedo boats. The pocket battleships, built in the mid-1930s, were experimental. They were specifically designed to raid commercial shipping on the high seas; six 11-inch guns and a top speed of 28 knots made these vessels more powerful than almost any enemy ship fast enough to catch them, and modern diesel engines gave them a range of 21,500 miles. The Germans called them *Panzerschiffe*—armored ships. The name pocket battleships was bestowed on them by the rest of the world because of their relatively small size: they were 609 feet long, with a displacement of 12,000 tons (a full-sized battleship was about 750 feet long, with a 35,000-ton displacement).

In addition to these vessels, two large battleships as well as one heavy cruiser were approaching completion. They would be the only reinforcements larger than a destroyer that Raeder would get.

The grand admiral was well aware that his forces would be outnumbered by the Royal Navy. Britain's fleet included

RAIDERS ON THE PROWL

15 battleships and battle cruisers, six aircraft carriers (Germany had none) and 58 cruisers. Raeder could not hope to defeat the Royal Navy, even by slow attrition. But by dispersing his forces far and wide, he hoped to keep the British ships tied up scouring the oceans in search of an elusive but dangerous assailant.

To supplement Germany's conventional warships and its fledgling U-boat force, Raeder planned to resurrect a weapon that had been employed with conspicuous success—although on a small scale—during the First World War: armed merchant raiders. Disguised to look like cargo vessels, these deadly marauders would prowl the seas like pirates of old, swooping down on solitary, unsuspecting ships, and capturing or sinking their prey before aid could be summoned. But not one of the raiders was ready when World War II began—Raeder's initial requests for the necessary armaments had been turned down.

The pocket battleships, on the other hand, were ready. Two of them, the *Deutschland* and the *Graf Spee (page 50)*, had been dispatched to the Atlantic a week before the start of the War. The first offensive moves of the surface war in the Atlantic would be conducted by these ships.

For three weeks, however, the *Deutschland* and the *Graf Spee* were held in check by Hitler in the hope that once Poland had been crushed, Great Britain and France would agree to a compromise peace. Only when it became clear that the Western Allies were intent upon seeing the War through did Hitler give permission for the pocket battleships to take action.

The *Graf Spee*, in her assigned operational zone south of the equator, struck first—and hard. On September 30, she overtook the British merchantman *Clement* off the coast of Brazil. The *Clement*'s captain, F. C. P. Harris, mistook the *Graf Spee* for the British cruiser *Ajax*, and repaired to his cabin to change into a clean white uniform so that he might greet his compatriots in proper style. He had hardly arrived back on the bridge when a seaplane from the *Graf Spee*, bearing an identifying Iron Cross, attacked the *Clement* and severely damaged her.

Captain Harris gave orders to lower the lifeboats and abandon ship. Taken aboard the *Graf Spee*, he was greeted politely by Captain Hans Langsdorff, who apologized but announced that he was going to have to sink the *Clement*. While Harris looked on, the *Graf Spee* opened fire. "She's a damned tough ship," he exclaimed as he watched the *Clement* go down.

Langsdorff then had his crew repaint the *Graf Spee*'s mast to match the distinctive coloration—light with dark trim—of a French warship. Within the next 17 days, benefiting from his ship's disguise, he sank three more British ships: the merchantman *Newton Beech* and two freighters, the *Ashlea* and the *Huntsman*.

He was off to a brilliant start. Not only was he capturing and sinking enemy ships one after another, but he was also disrupting the Royal Navy's dispositions: almost two dozen warships that were urgently needed for duties elsewhere had been diverted to the South Atlantic to hunt for the elusive *Graf Spee*.

On October 22, Langsdorff sank the British motor vessel *Trevanion*. By now, a full-scale search for the raider was under way; the hunters included two British vessels—the aircraft carrier *Ark Royal* and the battle cruiser *Renown*—and the French battleship *Strasbourg*.

To avoid his pursuers, Langsdorff decided to sail around the tip of Africa and into the Indian Ocean. Off the coast of Madagascar, on November 15, he sank the British tanker *Africa Shell*, taking her captain prisoner but allowing the crew to escape ashore.

It appeared at this point that Langsdorff could pursue his predatory ways indefinitely. His single ship was almost impossible to track in the wide reaches of the Atlantic and Indian oceans.

By the end of November 1939, the *Graf Spee* was back in the Atlantic, sinking two British cargo ships, the *Doric Star* on December 2 and the *Tairoa* the following day. Langsdorff then set course for the broad estuary of the River Plate, which empties into the South Atlantic and is heavily traveled by ships bound for England from both Buenos Aires, Argentina, and Montevideo, Uruguay.

On the evening of December 7, the *Graf Spee* stopped and sank the British steamer *Streonshalh*—her ninth victim. A sack of secret documents that had been thrown overboard by the captain was recovered, and from these papers Langsdorff learned of the assembly points for British ships leaving the River Plate. Looking forward to some "fine target practice," he sped on toward the South American coast.

By December 12, the *Graf Spee* was in the Plate area awaiting a five-ship British convoy that Langsdorff knew was due to depart from Montevideo. At 5:52 a.m. on the morning of December 13, the pocket battleship's lookout reported two masts on the starboard horizon. Within a few minutes, the masts were revealed to belong to the British heavy cruiser *Exeter*. Behind the *Exeter* followed two light cruisers, the *Ajax* and the New Zealand warship *Achilles*. All three ships could travel at a speed approximately five knots faster than the *Graf Spee* could, but all had far less firing power than the German ship, which was equipped with 11-inch guns. The *Exeter* carried six 8-inch guns; the *Ajax* and the *Achilles* were armed with nothing larger than six-inchers.

Langsdorff faced a choice. Either he could turn away and avoid action, or he could ignore his orders—which had specifically forbidden a direct confrontation with enemy warships—and engage all three warships at once.

The day before, Commodore Henry Harwood, who was in command of the South American force of the Royal Navy, had warned his subordinate captains to be on the lookout for the *Graf Spee* and had issued orders to be followed in the event that any of his ships met up with her: "Attack at once by day or night."

Harwood's ships followed his orders without hesitation. The *Exeter* immediately began closing on the pocket battleship's starboard bow while the *Ajax* and the *Achilles* were pounding along to the northeast to get on Langsdorff's port bow. All three ships would soon be within the 15-mile range of the *Graf Spee*'s big guns.

The *Exeter* came in range first. A 670-pound shell killed the starboard torpedo tube crew and seriously damaged the control mechanisms of the *Exeter*'s guns as well as the communications to the engine room. Still the *Exeter* closed with the larger German ship. She had just straddled the *Graf Spee* with her 8-inch shells when a German 11-inch shell crashed aboard, ripping off the front of one of the *Exeter*'s gun turrets and destroying the wheelhouse. The *Exeter* began to turn, out of control. Captain F. S. Bell was wounded by the German fire, but he managed to set up a temporary command station. Using a compass that had been taken from one of the lifeboats and a chain of sailors to relay his commands to the aft steering station, where sweating men

struggled to turn the rudder by hand, Bell somehow managed to bring his ship back on course. But two more shells from the *Graf Spee* tore a huge hole in the *Exeter*'s side above the water line and ripped up the deck. Fires were now wreathing the *Exeter* in smoke.

Both the *Ajax* and the *Achilles* closed on the *Graf Spee* while traveling at maximum speed, a dangerous maneuver for the lightly armored cruisers but one that forced Langsdorff to divide his fire among his three adversaries. After one and a half hours of furious firing, Commodore Harwood ordered his ships to break off the action under cover of a smoke screen. The battered *Exeter* limped away toward the Falkland Islands, carrying with her 51 dead and many wounded. By good luck and skillful maneuvering, the *Ajax* and the *Achilles* had come through with less damage, although one shell had knocked out both of the after turrets

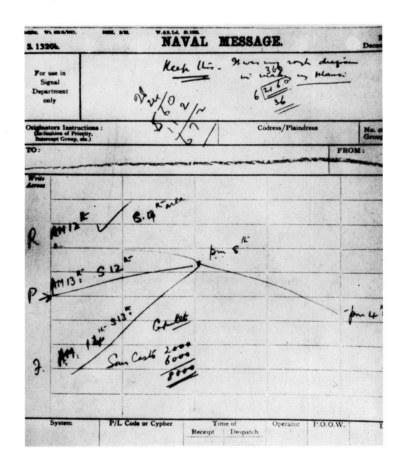

A diagram sketched on December 3, 1939, shows the calculations of Commodore Henry Harwood, commander of the Royal Navy's South America Division, who correctly divined the intentions of the German pocket battleship Graf Spee. Harwood estimated the Graf Spee's positions for December 4 and 8 and then figured that three options were open to her. She could arrive in Rio de Janeiro (R) by the morning of December 12, the River Plate (P) by the next morning, or the Falkland Islands (F) by the morning after that. The commodore decided the raider would be drawn to the Plate by its heavy shipping. When the Graf Spee arrived there, Harwood's three cruisers were waiting for her.

on the *Ajax,* and the captain of the *Achilles* had been wounded in both legs.

Aboard the *Graf Spee,* Langsdorff surveyed the damage that the British had inflicted upon his ship and reached a fateful decision. The pocket battleship had been hit 18 times; her galleys were wrecked and several secondary guns were out of commission. Thirty-seven members of his crew were dead—Langsdorff himself had been knocked temporarily unconscious by one blast. There were holes in the deck and sides of the ship, and her ammunition supply was depleted. The German captain decided that without repairs his ship could not possibly survive the long run for home through an aroused British fleet. So he turned west and headed for Montevideo, in neutral Uruguay.

The *Graf Spee* dropped anchor in Montevideo shortly before midnight on Wednesday, December 13. The *Ajax* and the *Achilles,* which had shadowed the *Graf Spee* at a respectful distance, stopped in the River Plate estuary well away from port and radioed for reinforcements. Langsdorff set himself to the tasks of burying his dead, treating his wounded and repairing his ship. With the chivalry that marked all his actions, he arranged for the release of the British prisoners who had been taken aboard the *Graf Spee* during past engagements; several responded by attending the funeral service for the dead crewmen of the *Graf Spee.* (Langsdorff had been so careful of human life during the voyage that although the *Graf Spee* had been responsible for sinking nine ships totaling some 50,000 tons, not a single Allied life had been lost.)

With the assistance of the German envoy in Montevideo, Langsdorff pressed for two weeks' grace in which to complete the repairs to his battered ship. The Uruguayans—fearful for their neutrality—granted him 72 hours. The British ambassador protested, but in truth the British did not want the *Graf Spee* to sail again until they could bring up heavy ships to cut off her escape. They inspired rumors that the carrier *Ark Royal* and the battle cruiser *Renown* had arrived off the coast of Montevideo. Langsdorff, unable to charter a private plane in the strongly anti-German city in order to survey the area for himself, believed that a large British force had arrived to blockade him. In fact, only the heavy cruiser *Cumberland* had joined the *Ajax* and the *Achilles* outside the harbor. Other reinforcements were still hundreds of miles away.

Langsdorff considered retreating up the Plate to Buenos Aires, where there was much pro-German sympathy, but he rejected that course because of the shallowness of the channel. Instructions from Berlin, approved by Hitler, ordered him to prevent capture of his ship at all costs. But time was running short.

On Sunday, the 17th of December, a launch was seen making repeated trips back and forth between the *Graf Spee* and a German merchantman, the *Tacoma,* which was anchored nearby in the Montevideo harbor. Slowly it became evident that most of the crew members of the pocket battleship were being transferred to the merchant ship.

Then, a few minutes after six in the evening, with battle ensigns flying, the *Graf Spee* left her mooring and moved out through the breakwater, closely followed by the *Tacoma.* Just outside the three-mile limit, they were joined by two Argentinian tugboats. The smaller vessels moved away, and the *Graf Spee* edged slightly out of the main channel. Then, as the sun went down, an enormous flash illuminated the pocket battleship and was followed by a series of explosions and billowing clouds of smoke. Langsdorff had scuttled his ship.

The *Graf Spee* burned for four days. It was two more days before the structure was cool enough for anyone to go aboard to investigate. By this time Captain Langsdorff was already dead. He had taken his crew to Buenos Aires in the *Tacoma* and the tugboats. There, in his room at the Naval Arsenal on December 20, he unrolled a large flag—not the swastika but the ensign of the old Imperial German Navy—lay down on it and shot himself. Left behind was a letter to the German ambassador to Argentina, Baron von Therman, explaining his action: "For a Captain with a sense of honor, it goes without saying that his personal fate cannot be separated from that of his ship."

A month before the *Graf Spee*'s dramatic end, her sister ship, the *Deutschland,* had been ordered home to Kiel after running up only a modest score in the North Atlantic. Two merchant ships had been sunk—one British, one Norwegian—and a third, the American freighter *City of Flint,* had been captured. The *Flint* episode had set off a furor in the United States and other neutral nations. The *Deutschland*'s captain put a special crew aboard the American ship, and they took her to Murmansk, a neutral Russian port above the Arctic Circle. The Russian authorities—abiding by their non-aggression pact with Germany—refused to intern the German crew and restore the ship to the Americans, as international law required, or even to allow the American ambassador to visit her. But when the Germans then tried to take the *Flint* to Germany through Norwegian waters, the Norwegians intercepted her and returned the *Flint* to her American crew.

Following this one sortie, Hitler ordered the *Deutschland's* name changed to the *Lützow*—after a Prussian hero of the Napoleonic Wars. The Führer was paranoid to the point of sleeplessness over the possible fate of his major ships when they were at sea. He considered the harm to national morale should a ship named the *Deutschland*—Germany—be lost. As the *Lützow*, the pocket battleship later was twice damaged by British torpedoes off Norway; she never returned to the raiding game in the Atlantic.

By the end of the winter of 1940, although German raiders had sunk only 11 ships totaling 57,000 tons, they had succeeded in their primary purpose. They had forced the British to disperse their merchant shipping and they had preoccupied and diverted the vastly larger Royal Navy. At one point 22 British cruisers, carriers and battleships, organized into nine separate hunting groups, were pursuing the elusive *Deutschland* and *Graf Spee*.

In the meantime, Germany's two small battle cruisers, the *Scharnhorst* and the *Gneisenau*, had kept another heavy British force occupied in the North Sea, sinking a British armed merchant cruiser, the *Rawalpindi*, in November 1939. But Germany's limited surface navy was heavily damaged in the Norwegian campaign during the following spring. Both the *Scharnhorst* and the *Gneisenau* were put out of action, as was the *Lützow*. The heavy cruiser *Blücher*, the light cruisers *Leipzig* and *Karlsruhe* and 10 German destroyers were sunk. With U-boats still not available in sufficient numbers to have a serious impact on Allied shipping, Admiral Raeder's navy needed an effective weapon to pursue its mercantile war.

One such weapon was now at hand. During the winter of 1939-1940, in Hamburg and in Germany's Baltic ports, six nondescript old freighters were converted into armed raiders on Admiral Raeder's orders. Eventually nine such ships, disguised as inoffensive neutral merchantmen, would slip through the North Sea passages into the Atlantic. From there they roamed the seas in every quarter of the globe in search of prey.

Over the next three and a half years this ragtag collection of marauders would sink 130 ships totaling 850,000 tons—almost three times the merchant tonnage sunk by Germany's conventional warships.

The *Atlantis (page 27)*, the first and, as it turned out, the most successful of these secret raiders, put to sea from Kiel on March 31, 1940. Originally a Hansa Line freighter named the *Goldenfels*, the *Atlantis* had been disguised to look like an auxiliary warship of neutral Russia. Her scouting seaplane was painted with Russian markings, and her deck crew wore an assortment of clothing that could, at a distance, pass for Russian uniforms.

In the *Atlantis'* holds were stored 400 tons of food, 3,000 tons of oil to fuel her diesels, 1,200 tons of fresh water and ample stocks of ammunition to feed her formidable armament. Six 5.9-inch guns, another six antiaircraft guns, one 75mm cannon and four torpedo tubes lurked behind hinged bulkheads that would drop away at the turn of a lever, and nearly 100 mines nestled in the stern. The crew of 347—large enough to provide skeleton crews for captured vessels—was commanded by Captain Bernhard Rogge.

The *Atlantis* could—and did—alter her appearance and her flag at frequent intervals. Like the other German raiders, she had telescopic funnels and masts, quickly removable derricks, and dummy deck cargoes that enabled her to change disguises in a matter of hours.

The *Atlantis'* first kill was typical of many more to come. By April 25, 1940, she was south of the equator. Few Russian ships could be expected to be traveling in the area, so Captain Rogge transformed his raider into the Japanese cargo and passenger ship *Kasii Maru*. Once the outline of the German ship had been suitably changed, the majority of the crew was kept belowdecks while the remaining members—selected because they were short and blackhaired, and dressed in dark trousers with white shirts hanging outside—danced attendance upon a tall, blonde "passenger" who was wheeling a baby carriage. Thus elaborately disguised, the *Atlantis* cruised along the fringes of the route from Cape Town to Freetown, on the prowl for unsuspecting merchant ships traveling alone.

On May 3, the British cargo ship *Scientist* was spotted, bound from Durban, South Africa, to Liverpool with a cargo of grain and chromium. The *Scientist* refused at first to obey Rogge's instructions to stop, and her captain and crew were appalled when the friendly-looking freighter flying the Rising Sun flag suddenly lowered it, hoisted the Nazi colors and opened fire at a range of three miles. The very first salvo bracketed the *Scientist*. It was followed immediately by hits on the stern, the bridge and the radio cabin—but not before the radio operator, though wounded, managed to send the alarm signal QQQ ("I am being attacked by an unidentified enemy ship").

Another salvo from the *Atlantis* landed amidships, and the *Scientist* was doomed. The lifeboats were lowered and the wounded handed down. And the rest of the crew followed and began pulling away from the stricken ship. As twilight thickened, flames broke upward through the decks of the *Scientist* and lighted up the ocean for miles around. The *Atlantis* closed in, finished off the *Scientist* with torpedoes and took aboard the survivors.

This was the beginning of a remarkable odyssey for Captain Rogge and the *Atlantis*. In all, he kept his raider at sea for 20 months of hit-and-run warfare, occasionally rendezvousing with other German ships to share supplies and fuel, and using his radio only rarely to contact headquarters in Germany. To combat monotony on the long cruise, Rogge started a daily newspaper, organized a ship's orchestra, and encouraged songfests and amateur theatricals among the crew. He even devised a system of "leave on board" under which rotating groups of officers and men were relieved of duty for a week or more—except when "Battle Stations" sounded—and were free to enjoy themselves almost like passengers on a holiday excursion.

In those 20 months the *Atlantis* circled the earth, steamed 102,000 miles and captured or sank 22 ships—including the Egyptian ship *Zamzam* with 138 Americans on board *(pages 24-37)*. The luck of the *Atlantis* finally ran out in November 1941, off Ascension Island in the South Atlantic. A British cruiser sank her after refusing to believe her signals that she was an innocent British merchantman. But Rogge and most of his crew were rescued by a submarine that happened to be in the area.

Though they were under orders not to engage enemy warships, the disguised raiders usually held their own when battle was forced upon them. The smallest of the lot, the *Thor* —a converted 3,100-ton banana boat—fought two much larger British armed merchant cruisers to a standstill and sank a third. Two other raiders, the *Stier* and the *Kormmoran,* managed, before they went under, to sink the Allied ships that sank them.

Most of the raider captains made prisoners of the crews of the vessels they sank and found ways to transfer them to other ships for delivery to friendly or neutral ports. The exception was Captain Helmuth von Ruckteschell of the raider *Widder,* who became notorious for firing on Allied ships without warning—to prevent them from sending radio signals—and then abandoning the crews in open lifeboats in mid-Atlantic. One such lifeboat drifted for 70 days before it reached an island in the Bahamas. Of its seven original occupants, five had gone mad and jumped into the sea; but two lived to describe their ordeal. Ruckteschell was convicted of war crimes at Nuremberg in 1946 and spent the rest of his life in prison.

Almost all of the 130 ships sunk by the disguised raiders were sailing alone. By late fall of 1940, Admiral Raeder was ready to send his limited force of battleships after bigger game: the Atlantic convoys. In November, the pocket battleship *Admiral Scheer* slipped past Iceland into the northwest Atlantic—the first heavy German ship to be at large since the scuttling of the *Graf Spee* almost a year before.

The *Scheer* quickly found rich pickings: Convoy HX-84, made up of 37 merchant ships protected by a single British armed merchant cruiser, the converted passenger liner *Jervis Bay,* eastward bound from Halifax, Nova Scotia. On sighting the *Scheer,* Captain E. S. F. Fegen of the *Jervis Bay* made one of the heroic decisions of the Atlantic war. Instructing the convoy to scatter, Fegen headed his ship at full speed directly toward the German pocket battleship.

Diverted from the merchantmen, the *Scheer* opened fire with her 11-inch guns at 18,000 yards, well beyond the range of the British ship's six-inchers. The *Jervis Bay* was hit again and again. But still firing those guns that had not been destroyed, she closed to within a mile before being sunk. The engagement had taken only 22 minutes, but it gave the convoy time to scatter.

The *Scheer* raced off into the gathering darkness after the fleeing merchant ships. Of the 37, the Germans found only six; they sank five of these.

The sixth ship—the tanker *San Demetrio*—was to provide a saga of her own. Shelled and set on fire, the *San Demetrio* was abandoned by her crew, who knew that within hours the cargo of gasoline was likely to explode.

But the following day, after surviving a bitter Atlantic gale, one of the lifeboats from the *San Demetrio,* under the command of the second officer, came upon the drifting tanker, which was still on fire but still intact. The survivors decided to go back on board.

When asked later why anybody would want to return to a blazing tanker, Able Seaman Calum MacNeil replied, "She was the only thing we could see in all the wide circle of ocean and she looked good. She might blow up at any time, but that was a quick and painless death compared to this slow freezing and sickness . . . and besides, she was our own ship."

For three days and three nights on sizzling decks and smoldering debris, the crew fought the fires and worked fever-

Oil-soaked crew members of the British destroyer Glowworm, just sunk by the German heavy cruiser Admiral Hipper, wallow on a nearly swamped lifeboat while being hoisted aboard by the raider's crew. The Glowworm was caught alone off the Norwegian coast by the Hipper and four destroyers on April 8, 1940, after parting company with the battle cruiser Renown to search for a sailor who had fallen overboard. Before going down, she managed to ram the Hipper.

ishly to repair the *San Demetrio*'s disabled machinery. At length they got the engines turning again, and the second officer, using a school atlas to navigate, and steering by the blackened stump that was all that remained of the ship's wheel, set a course for Liverpool at a speed of nine knots. On the 15th of November, 10 days after she had been left to sink, the *San Demetrio* made port.

By this time the *Scheer,* aware that the Royal Navy would soon be on her trail, had steamed off for the South Atlantic and the Indian Ocean. Before the *Scheer* returned home five months later, she had sunk 16 ships. More important, the attack on Convoy HX-84—while not a complete success because of Captain Fegen's courageous sacrifice of the *Jervis Bay*—had severely shaken British faith in the existing convoy system. The Admiralty decided that in the future an effort would be made to assign a battleship escort to every major convoy—thus thinning out the Royal Navy's battle squadrons even further.

In January 1941, while the *Scheer* was still at sea, Admiral Raeder also dispatched the *Scharnhorst* and the *Gneisenau* past the British blockade and into the Atlantic. Operating as a team, the two German battle cruisers destroyed 22 ships in two months, including 13 in two days on the Halifax run. The toll might have been higher except for the Germans' reluctance to risk battle and the possible loss of capital ships. On two occasions they turned away from large convoys escorted by single, aged British battleships.

In late March, after successfully evading the British Home Fleet again, the *Scharnhorst* and the *Gneisenau* put into port at Brest in German-occupied France, and the *Scheer* returned to Kiel.

The combined depredations of Germany's heavy warships, disguised raiders and submarines were severely straining Great Britain's resources. Losses in the Atlantic in March 1941 reached 350,000 tons—a new high for the War and a rate that Britain could not long survive. Moreover, Admiral Raeder was now preparing to launch his most ambitious strike of all.

The new battleship *Bismarck,* which had been under construction at Hamburg since 1936, was now ready for sea. Raeder planned to send her into the North Atlantic as the mainstay of a task force powerful enough to attack any convoy, no matter how strong its escort. The *Bismarck* would be joined by the new heavy cruiser *Prinz Eugen* and by the *Scharnhorst* and the *Gneisenau,* which were to sail out from Brest.

The *Bismarck* was Germany's most powerful battleship, yet designed with a grace and elegance that evoked a sense of pride and resurging nationalism in every German who saw her. Though listed at 35,000 tons to comply with the limits of the London Treaty of 1935, the *Bismarck* actually displaced more than 42,000 tons when empty. Measuring 823 feet from her impressively flared bows to her stern and 120 feet wide at the beam, she carried eight 15-inch guns and six aircraft, and was capable of making 30 knots. Most important perhaps, her sides and turrets were protected by 12.6 inches of specially hardened steel.

When the *Bismarck* was launched on St. Valentine's Day, 1939, Adolf Hitler was there to tell a cheering crowd that he hoped her future crew would demonstrate the same unbending determination as the Iron Chancellor for whom she had been named.

After spending more than two years in fitting and shakedown cruises, the *Bismarck* went to war under the command of a cool and experienced gunnery and engineering expert, Captain Ernst Lindemann. The average age of the crew of more than 2,000 was 20. Like the *Bismarck,* most of them were on their first voyage.

Operation *Rheinübung,* or Rhineland Exercise, the code name that Raeder gave his secret plan for the *Bismarck* task force, suffered delays and setbacks. The *Scharnhorst* had developed engine trouble and would have to miss the operation. The *Gneisenau* had been severely damaged in an air attack on Brest. At Churchill's urging, the Royal Air Force had been giving the harbor special attention, and on April 6, 1941, a torpedo bomber piloted by a Canadian, Flying Officer Kenneth Campbell, swept in low to score a hit on the stern of the *Gneisenau.* Seconds later, Campbell's plane was shot to pieces, but the *Gneisenau,* with a smashed propeller shaft and two engine rooms flooded, had been knocked out of action for six months.

No other major ships were available. Admiral Günther Lütjens, whom Raeder had chosen to command Operation *Rheinübung,* now counseled postponement—at least for several months until the powerful new battleship *Tirpitz,* a sister to the *Bismarck*, could be completed. But Raeder was adamant: the *Bismarck* and the new cruiser *Prinz Eugen* would have to go it alone.

Raeder had wanted to launch *Rheinübung* late in April, before the northern nights became too short. But minor damage to the *Prinz Eugen*, caused by a mine, meant further delay. It was not until the evening of May 18, 1941, that the two ships left Gotenhafen, on the Baltic Sea, to attempt the breakout into the Atlantic.

For the first time in the War, German warships had orders to engage the enemy fleet if necessary. Raeder had cleared his plan with Hitler, but knowing the Führer's paranoid fear of losing major ships—"On land I am a hero. At sea, I am a coward"—the admiral did not tell Hitler that the *Bismarck* and the *Prinz Eugen* had sailed until it was already too late to call them back.

The British Admiralty knew about the ships' departure before Hitler did. Coded sighting reports reached London by radio from Sweden and from an alert member of the Resistance in Norway. On May 21, a British reconnaissance plane photographed the *Bismarck* and the *Prinz Eugen* in a fjord just south of Bergen, Norway, where they had paused to take on additional fuel supplies. Two days later another

reconnaissance flight indicated that the ships had departed.

By this time, Admiral Sir John Tovey, commander-in-chief of the Home Fleet at Scapa Flow, was moving to intercept the Germans. Tovey sent a squadron made up of the new battleship *Prince of Wales*, the battle cruiser *Hood* and six destroyers, all commanded by Vice-Admiral L. E. Holland, to guard the passages on either side of Iceland. The next day Tovey himself sailed in the battleship *King George V*, in company with the carrier *Victorious*, the battle cruiser *Repulse*, and a screen of destroyers and light cruisers.

Lütjens had circled far to the north under the cover of stormy weather and was picking his way cautiously down the Greenland icepack west of Iceland. There, in the Denmark Strait, the *Bismarck* and the *Prinz Eugen* were discovered in the early evening of May 23 by a patrolling British cruiser, the *Suffolk*.

With her new 13-mile range radar, the *Suffolk*, accompanied by her sister ship, the *Norfolk*, shadowed the larger German ships. Meanwhile, Admiral Holland's squadron raced through the night to confront them, with his flagship, the *Hood*, leading the way.

The "mighty *Hood*," as the British called her, was the most famous warship afloat. To most of the world, the battle cruiser *was* the British Navy. She had spent the years between the wars proudly showing the Union Jack from Zanzibar to San Francisco, her dignified beauty admired by the millions who saw her and by the hundreds of thousands of visitors—from schoolboys to statesmen—who were invited to tour her decks.

Longer even than the *Bismarck*, at 860 feet, and almost as heavy, the *Hood* had an armament of eight 15-inch guns, comparable to that of her German foe. But by now the *Hood* was getting old. The only notable action she had seen was the shelling of the French fleet at Mers-el-Kebir in North Africa, shortly after the fall of France in 1940.

If the *Hood* was too old for the task ahead, her consort, the battleship *Prince of Wales*, may have been just the opposite. So new was she that gun crews and civilian dock workers were still struggling to make the 14-inch batteries work properly when the ship sailed northwest from Scapa Flow toward Iceland.

Whatever the odds, there was no question that Holland's squadron must find the enemy ships and do everything

An aerial photograph taken from a British Spitfire flying over Norway's Grimstad fjord on May 21, 1941, betrays the powerful new German battleship Bismarck (lower left). The picture was so important that the pilot who took it returned to Scotland, had prints developed there, and then took off for London. When his plane ran short of fuel, he landed about 120 miles away from the city, managed to borrow a car, and drove the rest of the way—through the blackout, at 50 mph.

possible to detain them until Admiral Tovey's force could arrive in support. Shortly after midnight on May 24, Holland signaled "Prepare for Action," and battle ensigns were broken out on both of his great ships.

The anxious hours passed. Aboard the *Prince of Wales* the actor Esmond Knight was serving as a lieutenant. He later wrote: "After minutes of staring at the blank distance, suddenly—and one could scarcely believe one's eyes—there appeared the topmasts of two ships! Again that phrase was shouted by the first man who could find his voice—'Enemy in sight!'"

Knight watched, fascinated, as the *Prince of Wales*'s great turrets swiveled around and the German warships came nearer. "There they were, in deep sharp silhouette on the horizon—*Bismarck* and *Prinz Eugen*, steaming in smokeless line ahead, unperturbed and sinister. 'Ye gods!—what a size!' I heard someone mutter."

The order to fire was flashed at 5:52 a.m. "Almost immediately after there were the great orange flashes and huge clouds of black smoke belching from the for'ard turrets of the *Hood* as she fired her first salvo."

Then it was the *Prince of Wales*'s turn. "Two more moments of unendurable ecstasy, then that pulverising, crash-ing roar, which for a second seems to knock one sense-less—we had opened fire! We were blinded by a dense sheet of flame which rose before us, mixed with clouds of black, bitter-smelling smoke."

The wait was even more unendurable when the German warships, their backs to the icecap, returned the fire. Knight saw "those brilliant flashes and the same jet-black smoke belching from *Bismarck*." The incoming shells hurtled toward them with a sound like the "approach of an underground train, getting louder and louder and filling the air, suddenly to cease as the first great spouts of water rose just astern of *Hood*." The thundering shells from the *Bismarck* were punctuated by an "ear-splitting crack" as the *Prinz Eugen*'s high explosive shells, "exploding practically overhead, rained showers of shrapnel onto the decks and into the sea around."

Then, aboard the *Hood,* the worst happened: a shell struck the magazine. As Knight and the others on the *Prince of Wales* watched in horror, "a great spouting explosion issued from the center of the *Hood*, enormous reaching tongues of pale-red flame shot into the air, while dense clouds of whitish-yellow smoke burst upwards, gigantic

Swordfish torpedo bombers on the carrier Victorious are readied for a May 25, 1941, foray against the Bismarck. The canvas-covered biplanes flew more than 100 miles to hit the massive battleship. "It was incredible," said one German officer, "to see such obsolete-looking planes having the nerve to attack a fire-spitting mountain like the Bismarck." Equally remarkable, none of the slow-moving Swordfish were shot down and all of them managed to return safely to the Victorious.

pieces of brightly burning debris being hurled hundreds of feet in the air. I just did not believe what I saw—Hood had literally been blown to pieces." Of 1,419 men on the Hood, only three survived.

The Prince of Wales now became the target for both the Bismarck and the Prinz Eugen. The British ship's 14-inch guns were working only erratically, and she was hit several times in rapid succession. One shell wrecked her bridge, killing or wounding everyone there except Captain John Leach and the chief signalman (Esmond Knight was blinded). Leach prudently withdrew his ship out of range of the Bismarck's guns and joined the Suffolk and the Norfolk in the task of shadowing the enemy.

Ernst Lindemann, captain of the Bismarck, now urged Admiral Lütjens to return to Germany with both his ships. The element of surprise was now gone. The Royal Navy knew the Germans' position, and warships from all over the Atlantic would be converging on them, primed for revenge. Lindemann's advice was not taken, although Lütjens did modify his plans. He detached the Prinz Eugen to hunt for enemy merchant vessels while the Bismarck made for the French port of Saint-Nazaire and repairs. The Bismarck had been hit by only two English shells, but one of them had ruptured a fuel tank. She was trailing oil and, until the tank could be repaired in dry dock, her range would be reduced. If he could not shake off the Suffolk, the Norfolk and the Prince of Wales, Lütjens planned a nasty surprise for them. He radioed Berlin to ask that a line of six U-boats be formed between himself and the French coast, over which he would draw his pursuers.

During the night that followed, the Bismarck's antiaircraft guns fended off an attack by torpedo-carrying Swordfish planes from the carrier Victorious. Then for six hours, the Suffolk's radar lost track of the Bismarck. But Admiral Lütjens, not realizing that his pursuers had lost contact, chose this time to send a long radio message to Berlin describing the engagement in the Denmark Strait. The message took more than 30 minutes to transmit. That was more than enough time for British direction-finding radio sets to zero in on the Bismarck again. Then the British navigators erroneously plotted their quarry 200 miles north of her actual position. The Bismarck lengthened her lead while the British force steamed in the wrong direction, wasting time and precious fuel.

Incredibly, the German radio traffic continued, and British cryptanalysts were able to decode enough of it to determine that Lütjens had the Bismarck on course for Brest. On the scent once more, Tovey swung his force to the southeast. Most of his destroyers and cruisers, by now low on fuel, had to head for home. The damaged Prince of Wales was also forced to give up the chase. But the battleship Rodney, slower than the Bismarck, but with nine powerful 16-inch guns, had been diverted from convoy duty to join the chase. Still more British ships were steaming up from the south to try to cut off the Bismarck. Among them were the carrier Ark Royal, the battle cruiser Renown and the cruiser Sheffield, all from the Royal Navy's Force H, stationed at Gibraltar. The net was closing in, if the Bismarck could only somehow be slowed down.

At midmorning on May 26 a long-range Catalina flying boat, dispatched from Northern Ireland, sighted the Bismarck some 700 miles from the coast of France. That afternoon the Ark Royal launched 15 of her Swordfish biplanes armed with torpedoes with magnetic exploders. But by mistake they attacked the cruiser Sheffield, which had gone ahead to scout. Only some wild maneuvering by the Sheffield in the stormy seas, and the fact that most of the magnetic exploders on the torpedoes were faulty and exploded prematurely, prevented the British pilots from sinking one of their own ships.

Before darkness fell, the Ark Royal's planes had enough time to make one more attack. It would be the last chance to get the Bismarck before the battleship reached friendly cover. This time, as the planes took off in gale-driven rain, they carried torpedoes that were equipped with the older, more reliable contact exploders.

The Bismarck blazed away at the incoming Swordfish with 56 antiaircraft guns. But the flimsy canvas covering that made the old-fashioned planes appear to be so fragile actually helped them to survive. Shell splinters tore the canvas to shreds but did not cause the fatal shattering that might have occurred with a metal fuselage.

Two torpedoes struck the Bismarck. One did no damage, but the other smashed into the steering engine room. That hit was to prove disastrous to the great battleship. The

Bismarck had been in a hard turn to port when the torpedo struck; now both her rudders were jammed at a 15-degree angle. Every combination of her engines served only to bring her bow plunging into the wind, toward the north-west—and the approaching Home Fleet.

Aboard the *Bismarck* a night of despair followed. A flotilla of five fresh destroyers appeared to harass the stricken giant. Admiral Lütjens offered to reward the Iron Cross on the spot to any volunteer who could blast free the jammed rudders in the flooded engine steering room. But every effort failed. Even a message from the Führer: "The whole of Germany is with you," did little to revive the flagging spirits of the *Bismarck's* exhausted crew.

Morning brought more squalling rain, and the British battleships *King George V* and *Rodney* were closing in rapidly from the northwest, supported by the heavy cruisers *Norfolk* to the north and *Dorsetshire* to the south. At 8:47 a.m. the *Rodney* opened fire from 12 miles away, followed immediately by the *King George V*. The *Bismarck* returned their fire, but she was barely maneuverable.

The *Rodney's* third salvo destroyed one of the *Bismarck's* forward turrets. Splinters swept the bridge. The *Norfolk* and the *Dorsetshire* joined the fight. Shell after shell smashed into the *Bismarck's* superstructure. Her fire control machinery was demolished. The *King George V* and the *Rodney* closed to four miles, then to two miles—point-blank range. Observers saw shell after shell from the British ships strike home. By 10 a.m. the *Bismarck* was still afloat and under way, but her guns were silent.

At 10:15 a.m., Lieut. Commander Gerhard Junack, the *Bismarck's* chief turbine engineer, was told that the ship was sinking. With difficulty, he made his way topside. "There was no electric light," he wrote later, "only the red glow from numerous fires; smoke fumes billowed everywhere; crushed doors and hatches littered the deck, and men were running here and there, apparently aimlessly: it seemed highly unlikely that one would survive."

Assuming command of the crew milling about on the deck, Junack told the men "to make their last preparations and then gave a few simple orders—stay together in the water, keep calm, don't give up hope, and be careful when interrogated by the enemy. After a triple 'Sieg Heil!,' I ordered 'abandon ship.' Hardly were we free of the ship when it keeled over to port, rolling the deck-rail under and bringing the bilge-keel out of the water. A pause—then *Bismarck* turned keel-up, slowly, the bows rose in the air, and, stern first, *Bismarck* slid down to the bottom."

Of the more than 2,000 officers and men who had sailed from Gotenhafen nine days earlier, only 110 were rescued. Neither Admiral Lütjens nor Captain Lindemann was among these survivors.

Thus ended Operation *Rheinübung*, and with it the major effort of Germany's surface navy in the Battle of the Atlantic. Within a month the Royal Navy—again aided by information from the cryptanalysts who were decoding German maritime wireless traffic—located and destroyed half a dozen supply ships that were vital to sustained German operations in the Atlantic. A few disguised merchant raiders remained at large until the end of 1943, but for the most part they limited their clandestine work to the Indian and Pacific oceans.

The *Prinz Eugen* eluded the British hunters and reached Brest four days after the *Bismarck* went down. But the French port was within easy reach of the increasingly dangerous RAF. In February 1942, the *Prinz Eugen*, the *Scharnhorst* and the *Gneisenau*—screened by no fewer than 60 smaller escort ships and 250 aircraft—succeeded in a surprise daylight dash up the English Channel and under the cliffs of Dover to the relative safety offered by German ports on the North Sea.

By this time, the *Bismarck's* sister battleship, the *Tirpitz*, had joined the German fleet. But her effectiveness was limited. Hitler, who was still haunted by the loss of the *Bismarck*, had decreed that all of his remaining major ships must "avoid any unnecessary risks"; none could sail without first obtaining his express approval. By now also, Germany's supply of the high-quality fuel oil that was needed to drive a battleship's turbines was running low enough to necessitate careful rationing.

Admiral Raeder stationed the *Tirpitz* in northern Norway as the centerpiece of a force that for two years would help to make the "Murmansk Run" a murderous gauntlet for Allied convoys trying to bring supplies to Russia. But never again would the big ships venture into the Atlantic to sink Allied vessels.

That was left to the submarines.

SUICIDE OF A MARAUDER

With a Nazi ensign whipping at the stern, the new pocket battleship Graf Spee *gets ready to join an international naval review at Spithead, England, in 1937.*

THE GRAF SPEE'S LAST DAYS

In the Graf Spee's marauding days, crewmen watch from the pocket battleship's deck as another of the raider's merchant victims goes down.

One of the most dramatic episodes of the early days of the Battle of the Atlantic, the attack by three British ships on the powerful pocket battleship *Graf Spee,* gave a few days of unaccustomed prominence and diplomatic intrigue to the neutral port of Montevideo, Uruguay. The damaged warship—with 57 wounded and 37 dead on board—had sought refuge there, but found herself instead in a trap. British vessels blocked her exit and the Uruguayans refused to extend the 24-hour layover permitted by international law beyond a 72-hour grace period granted ships needing repairs.

This suited the British, for at the end of the 96 hours the *Graf Spee* would either have to limp out of port with her repairs incomplete and engage their warships, or remain at anchor, subject to international law that would require her to be seized and her crew interned. Then the British discovered that she was not so damaged as they had believed. Anxiously, they cast about for a scheme to prevent her from escaping before the 96 hours were up.

Since international law forbade a warship of a belligerent nation to leave a neutral port for a day after the departure of a merchant ship of the opposing side, British diplomats rushed a note to the Uruguayan government stating that one of their cargo vessels would be sailing in a few hours. The government accepted the note, but did no more than send a small tug to deter the warship if she too set sail.

It was plain to the chief of British intelligence that something drastic had to be done. But time was running out. He had a brainstorm: "Let us lead the Germans to believe that we have heavy reinforcements arriving." The trick would be to leak the information to the Germans, via a fake telephone call to the British ambassador—whose line was known to be tapped by German intelligence—and a planted story in a newspaper in neighboring Argentina.

But the captain of the *Graf Spee,* Hans Langsdorff ("a high-class person," in the words of Winston Churchill), knew there was no escape. The steps he took to save his honor and keep his ship from being seized form the gripping finale to the story of the *Graf Spee.*

At a Montevideo cemetery, Captain Hans Langsdorff uses a naval, not Nazi, salute in final tribute to members of his crew who were killed in action.

Part of a crowd of a quarter of a million jams
the quays and harbor docks at Montevideo
on Sunday, the Graf Spee's last day in port. The
spectators expected to be witnesses of a
great sea battle, but the battle never came off.

Smoke and flames envelop the once-mighty *Graf Spee,* scuttled by her captain in the River Plate. The fire burned for four days, and the structure was so hot that for two more days the hulk could not be boarded.

Waving to friendly crowds ashore, crewmen from the Graf Spee depart for Buenos Aires on an Argentine tugboat that made its way up the shallow River Plate. Most of the seamen were interned in Argentina, but some managed later to escape and get back to Germany.

The crew of the scuttled Graf Spee holds its final muster with Captain Hans Langsdorff (inside circle, hands on hips) in a courtyard of the Naval Arsenal in Buenos Aires. The captain spoke briefly to his crew, saluted them and then went off to his quarters in the arsenal. There he committed suicide.

Stiff-armed Nazi salutes honor Captain Langsdorff as his funeral cortege

accompanies his coffin to its grave in Buenos Aires' Chacarita Cemetery. A British merchant captain also attended, sent by the officers Langsdorff had captured.

Jubilant crewmen on the British cruiser Exeter celebrate their triumph over the Graf Spee. The Exeter bore the brunt of the fighting as the Graf Spee was chased into Montevideo. Afterward the British warship, badly damaged, withdrew to the Falkland Islands for repairs.

Through London's Admiralty Arch and past throngs of cheering civilians march the crews of three British cruisers—the Ajax, the Achilles and the Exeter—

that helped to bring about the Graf Spee's end. Their victory in the Battle of the River Plate boosted British morale in the dark early months of the War.

3

It was midnight in the North Atlantic, under a clear but moonless sky. A light southwest wind was blowing that would bring clouds before dawn, but there was no likelihood of rain squalls. Lieut. Commander Otto Kretschmer leaned contentedly against his U-boat's conning-tower rail and drew luxuriantly upon his newly lighted cigar.

So far, so good, he thought.

Kretschmer had left Wilhelmshaven during the last days of June 1940 in his new command, the 750-ton submarine *U-99*. He had made his way across the North Sea into the North Atlantic, then down past the Hebrides and on to his patrol area. At noon on July 5, he had radioed Admiral Dönitz' headquarters in Wilhelmshaven that he was in position to commence playing his part in the Battle of the Atlantic. It was now July 8. In the intervening days, he had sunk—with just one torpedo apiece—the Canadian steamer *Magog* and the Swedish ship *Bissen*, a neutral vessel that he felt sure was carrying supplies to Britain.

Kretschmer's crew were for the most part young, eager and well trained; they had reason to be confident. The captain could hear some of them now moving below, talking softly among themselves. Forward and aft the lookouts maintained their slow, rhythmic scanning of the horizon, the everlasting, painstaking vigil that kept the *U-99* alive and helped her to locate her prey.

Suddenly one of them froze, then waved and quietly called to Kretschmer. Immediately binoculars swung to the east as Kretschmer's half-finished cigar sizzled out its life in the sea at the end of a fiery arc. The whole boat was now seething with movement; at Kretschmer's command she began picking up speed until finally the diesels were thumping away at full power.

Heading out through the Western Approaches was the *U-99*'s first convoy, two columns of ships, with a destroyer on each side and one up ahead.

Kretschmer forced his vessel along at full speed for nearly two hours, to place her directly in the path of the convoy. Just after dawn he submerged to periscope depth and waited for the merchantmen to creep over him. He had long insisted the best way to attack a convoy was from the middle of it, and this was his first chance to test his theory.

Kretschmer could now hear the destroyers' whirring propellers, and the sound grew louder as the destroyer on the

"HAPPY TIME" FOR U-BOATS

convoy's portside approached him. She slid past the U-99's stern torpedo tube and turned hard toward the U-boat. Even as Kretschmer opened his mouth to order a dive, the escort zigzagged away and the leading ships of the convoy approached on either side.

There was no need to aim the U-99 at an enemy ship for, if the torpedoes were set correctly before firing, they would turn at any angle up to 90 degrees as soon as they left the tubes and head for the target. When the leading ships came abreast, Kretschmer gave the order to fire; the U-99 rocked under the recoil and all aboard held their breath waiting for the explosions. Meantime the captain gently nursed his boat farther back along a lane between ships of the convoy, waiting for his next targets to align themselves in his sights.

Interminably, the seconds passed as everyone counted. Nothing happened. Puzzled, Kretschmer waited and then fired again. This time the stern torpedo "hung" and went out late. It appeared to turn correctly, however, and once more all hands waited, counting. Nothing, nothing, nothing. Then at last came a bright flash from a big ship that could have been a liner. Of all the U-99's carefully aimed torpedoes, only the one that had hung had hit anything. It was clear that something was wrong with the torpedoes. Furious, Kretschmer housed the periscope, took the U-99 down deep and dropped astern of the convoy, intending to break off the attack. Suddenly he heard the propeller noises of an approaching destroyer. The sound drew closer, then receded, then grew louder again. The counterattack was on.

The U-99 was down to about 150 feet and moving steadily ahead when the first pattern of 10 charges exploded close around her. There was a noise as though a gigantic hammer had hit the hull; the boat rocked fiercely, throwing every movable object onto the control-room deck, and then she dropped 20 feet like a stone. Kretschmer let her slide all the way down to 350 feet.

Now the new members of his crew were hearing for the first time the sound that would chill their blood: the pinging of the British asdic, presaging hours of increasing danger and overpowering fear, which could terminate for all in asphyxiation or suffocation if they were pinned down too long. As Kretschmer and his crew listened, there was a rush of propellers overhead, then another wait, and then another violent upheaval as a second pattern of depth charges

crashed around them. The U-99 bucked and rolled, and all aboard her gripped stanchions and overhead pipes to stop themselves from being hurled to the deck. Then, as the U-boat steadied, electricians and engineers checked their equipment and reported the damage. Not much harm had been done yet, but it was as well to plan for a long ordeal. To save precious battery power, Kretschmer ordered all electrical equipment shut down except hydrophones, gyrocompass and minimal lighting. Speed was also reduced—for escape now could not be bought by speed. However fast the U-99 moved underwater, the escorts could move faster. There was nothing to do except sweat it out, and pray that the enemy above would lose track of them, run out of depth charges or return to the convoy.

Two hours after the attacks had begun, a sudden close explosion threw the U-99 sideways through the water. With the oxygen supply failing, Kretschmer ordered the crew to lie down; while they were still they would use as little air as possible. He also ordered them to put on their rubber breathing masks, which filtered the increasingly toxic air through alkali, a chemical that would purify it—but only for a short time.

The first lull came after six hours—six hours of ever-growing tension, of thunderous explosions that threatened to blow in the submarine's already badly battered sides, of repeated calls from the hydrophone operator ("Attacker above!"), followed always by the awful wait.

Suddenly the explosions stopped. Kretschmer left the control room to Lieutenant Klaus Bargsten, groped his way through the boat to check the state of his command, exchanged a few cool remarks with those of his crew who seemed in need of conversation, and then lay down in his cramped quarters in one corner of the wardroom. Then surprisingly, except to those who knew him well, the commander dropped off to sleep.

Kretschmer had dozed for 40 minutes when another pattern of depth charges exploded close by, rocking the U-99 so violently as to awaken him with a start. The ordeal was not yet over.

In some ways it was better for him than for the rest of the crew; in some ways it was worse. As the U-boat's commander, he had of course to think and to make decisions—and the thinking and the weighing of conditions kept his mind away from the more disastrous areas of contemplation where panic lurked. On the other hand, no matter what happened or how bad things became, he bore the responsibility for his crew and his vessel, and must present an appearance of total imperturbability.

Kretschmer picked up a book and settled back in the corner of the control room, in full view of the hydrophone operator. There was little chance that the book would even gain his attention, let alone hold it. But in the stillness that came over the whole boat when the men learned that the captain was sufficiently unconcerned by the situation to be reading a detective novel, Kretschmer had the opportunity to calculate the odds.

The odds did not appear to be favorable. Inevitably, the U-99's batteries would run down, and once the boat lost all speed, Kretschmer had two choices. Since no submarine can remain suspended in water like a cloud of seaweed, he could either use his compressed-air supply to bring the U-99 to the surface—where she risked being destroyed—or he could let her settle to the bottom, where she risked being crushed by water pressure.

But the most immediate problem was that of breathing. Already, some members of the crew were gasping, the air was tainted with carbon dioxide, and even after a comparatively short time, rubber mouthpieces taste foul and begin to chafe the tender skin of lips and gums. How long must they endure it, Kretschmer wondered; how long would they be *able* to endure it?

Another fact of life was now adding to their discomfort. Because feces are less dense than sea water, they rise to the surface when discharged; orders had been issued early on that no one was to use the "heads" and thus betray their position to the hunters above. Instead they used buckets. More and more, the atmosphere inside the U-99 was fouled, and when more explosions rocked her from side to side, the containers overturned and spilled their contents over the already strewn and cluttered control-room deck.

Worse still, if the hammering of depth-charge explosions continued, sea water might seep in through strained seams or cracked plates and reach the batteries—in which case, chlorine poisoning was the fate that awaited them all. It was at about this time in Kretschmer's cogitations that the hydrophone operator noticed that his captain was holding the novel upside down.

By now the U-99 had been submerged and under attack for more than 12 hours. The batteries were so weak that the U-boat was barely moving, and as a result she was now a full 150 feet below the safety level for submarines of her class. Some of the latest recruits to the U-boat service, who were making their first cruise, were beginning to wonder if they would not have been wiser to follow the courses chosen by their brothers or friends who had opted for less hazardous lines of duty as fighter pilots or paratroopers.

Having kept to the same course without the slightest deviation for 12 hours, Kretschmer decided to try to elude his pursuers by making a series of sharp turns.

His ruse worked; at 8:30 p.m. he noted, "I get the impression that they have lost me. The heavy swell . . . appears to have made their task very difficult."

The periodic thrumming of propellers and the thud of grouped explosions could still be heard, but the sounds were not so near now. As minute followed minute, the thuds grew fainter, and no longer did those sinister electronic pings stiffen the hairs on the backs of the men's necks. At 10:28 p.m., the warrant officer recorded yet another group of three depth charges dropped by the enemy, making a total of 107 in all. Then, as the explosion-free minutes lengthened to larger and larger fractions of an

A 19-year-old U-boat hero proudly examines an Iron Cross he has just received for participating in a successful Atlantic patrol. Submarine crews ranged in age from 18 to 22, and on the average were younger than men in the surface navy, which was crowded with reservists and old hands. Many came from vocational schools, where they had studied such vital subjects as diesel engines, electricity and mechanics.

hour, the men began to hope that the danger was over.

And so it proved. But the ordeal of the U-99's crew had still some time to run. For two and a half more hours they remained submerged. Convinced at last that the destroyers had gone, Kretschmer decided to take his U-boat up.

At 1 a.m., after almost 18 hours underwater, the U-99 broke surface on a calm, black North Atlantic night, and Kretschmer flung back the hatch and clawed his way up to the conning tower. Below, the diesels burst into life; the fans started to suck fresh, cool air down into the hull and blow out the last of the foul contamination. Then the rest of the officers and the crew poured up from below and lay gasping on the deck, intoxicated as much by the relaxation of tension as by the heady effects of pure air after such hours of near-asphyxiation.

They were still alive.

They were also still on duty and, having checked the fuel situation and their distance from their final destination at Lorient, the new U-boat base on the French coast, Kretschmer was delighted to find that there was no urgent need to desert the area. He later had reason to be pleased that he had lingered. Three days later, on July 12, he sank the Greek steamer Ia, and that same day the U-99 captured the Estonian freighter Merisaar. Kretschmer instructed the badly shaken skipper to head for Bordeaux, threatening him with dire penalties if he diverged by as much as one degree from the stated course. This was pure bluff, of course, but unfortunately for all aboard the skipper believed it, with the result that as soon as the Merisaar came within striking distance of the coast, she was seen by reconnaissance planes and sunk by one of the Focke-Wulf bombers that were attached to the U-boat command.

On July 18 the U-99 sank the British steamer Woodbury; the stricken ship folded in two and disappeared from sight within 20 seconds.

A few days later, the U-99 arrived at Lorient; she was one of the first U-boats to make the trip from the Baltic to the new base. Kretschmer and his crew were greeted at dockside by members of Dönitz' staff who were setting up his headquarters at Kerneval, a village near Lorient. But the men's personal belongings and dress uniforms had not yet arrived from Wilhelmshaven. They could hardly go on wearing the stained and stinking overalls they had worn during their ordeal, so they were all issued the only spare uniforms in the area—British battle dress left behind during the hasty evacuation from Dunkirk one month earlier.

Dressed in the uniforms of the enemy, the U-99's crew were inspected by no less a personage than Admiral Raeder, and at the conclusion of the inspection the admiral presented Kretschmer with the coveted Ritterkreuz—the Knight's Cross to the Iron Cross.

Kretschmer's success was just one high point of what the young U-boat commanders and their crews were later to call the "Happy Time." There were by now many "young wolves" who had demonstrated their worth—and many more coming along to follow their example. Prien was still perhaps the most famous, but Kretschmer was swiftly catching up with him, as were lieutenant commanders Herbert Schultze, Heinrich Liebe and Wolfgang Lüth.

Nevertheless, Dönitz was troubled. And nothing illustrates the reason for his concern better than the Kretschmer story. No one could have asked more of Kretschmer, but for all his daring and determination, the mission he had just completed represented a lost opportunity. He had spotted a convoy and attempted to attack it all by himself. Only one ship had been hit, and in the chase that ensued, Kretschmer had almost been done in by the convoy's escort. In the end, it had been a triumphant operation, but there clearly was something wrong with the system. Shipping losses to the submarines were rising dramatically—more than a quarter of a million tons of Allied ships had been sunk in the month of June. But the losses might well have been multiplied many times, if Dönitz could have deployed a more formidable U-boat fleet. There were too many convoys getting by unmolested and too many attacks that failed to realize their potential. If Britain was to be defeated, a much bigger effort would be needed. Dönitz had estimated that it would take 300 U-boats attacking in highly coordinated groups to force Britain out of the War.

The necessary U-boats would not be forthcoming for many months. Germany had started the War with 46 submarines, and a year later the number was exactly the same. Dönitz had been promised an intensified U-boat building program, but it would be late 1941 before he could count on a substantial increase in his submarine fleet. He was convinced that the only way to do serious damage to the enemy was by means of the wolf pack—a herd of U-boats converging on a convoy with such swiftness and deadly power that massive shipping losses could be inflicted.

The idea had taken root in his mind back in World War I. U-boats had fought alone in the conflict and had proved unable to penetrate the escort screen of effectively organized convoys and thus unable to inflict serious damage on the cargo ships. During that war, Dönitz had tried to institute a limited version of the wolf-pack strategy. In September 1918, he and another U-boat commander had planned a coordinated mission, described by Dönitz as "the first ever undertaken by two U-boats together," but the joint attack never came off, because the other submarine had been forced to put into port for repairs.

He had gone ahead alone, cautiously moving through a destroyer screen to attack a convoy of merchant ships. But Dönitz had scored only one hit, and his submarine had been fired on, with the loss of seven men.

The experience had taught Dönitz a lesson that he never forgot. "The greater the number of U-boats that could be brought simultaneously into the attack," he later wrote, "the more favorable would become the opportunities to each individual attacker."

In order for a wolf pack to accomplish its mission, efficient radio communications and a high degree of coordination were needed. The tactic called for several U-boats to spread out along known convoy routes. The first one to sight enemy ships would signal headquarters for reinforcements. That sub would continue to shadow the convoy and report its position until others arrived for the attack.

The high degree of coordination that was required would not have been possible in World War I. Because radio communications were insufficiently developed at the time, surfaced U-boats had to spend precious time rigging up cumbersome, undependable aerials before they could signal each other. But by the outbreak of World War II, radio communications had been vastly improved, enabling surfaced U-boats to talk to each other and to communicate with headquarters over distances of hundreds of miles.

For the first few months of World War II, there were not enough operational U-boats to implement the wolf-pack strategy. But Dönitz estimated that by March of 1940, he would have eight U-boats operating in the Atlantic and six in the North Sea. The time seemed ripe to test the strategy on a limited scale. Then on March 4, Dönitz received a message from Admiral Raeder's headquarters that upset his plans. "All further sailing of U-boats stopped forthwith," the message said. The reason: the invasion of Norway was on, and the entire U-boat fleet would be needed.

The next few months were a time of great frustration for Dönitz. The invasion of Norway proved to be a highly successful campaign for the German Army, but it was a disaster for the Navy. Among the 30 vessels lost were six U-boats. Moreover, the submarine fleet had been rendered all but useless by the failure of torpedoes to keep to their set depth or to detonate properly.

Time after time the submarines got themselves into position to fire, only to have the torpedoes explode at the wrong moment or fail to go off. Prien had come upon a row of enemy transports lying quietly at anchor just off the Norwegian coast. He fired eight torpedoes at the motionless row of ships, and did not score a single hit. Another U-boat had fired on two destroyers with like results. A salvo of three torpedoes had missed one British cruiser, while a salvo aimed at another cruiser had exploded prematurely. An analysis of a series of disastrous torpedo firings showed that out of 14 attacks on a cruiser, 10 on a destroyer and 10 on transports, only one ship—a transport—was sunk.

Dönitz spent most of the Norwegian campaign worrying about the torpedo crisis. The problem proved to be a faulty magnetic firing device, which was setting torpedoes off at the wrong time or not at all. The solution arrived at was to arm the torpedoes with impact firing devices, mechanisms that would trigger an explosion when a target was hit. But installing these devices took time; and the entire German submarine fleet had to be laid up for two months while the torpedoes were rearmed.

With the Norwegian campaign over and the torpedo problem solved, Dönitz and his U-boats could turn their attention to the Battle of the Atlantic again. Their prospects there were greatly improved with the fall of France that summer. The U-boats were moved down from their Baltic bases to Atlantic ports in Occupied France, shortening the distance to the battle areas by 450 miles. Not only could

A wartime U.S. naval intelligence diagram of a U-boat, prepared during the Battle of the Atlantic, provides side and overhead views of the submarine's interior, with living and working compartments carefully labeled. The abbreviation "mag." indicates the ammunition magazine, "w.l." waterline. Inspection of captured enemy submarines later revealed that the drawing was accurate; but naval intelligence erred in one respect: they spelled the word "diesel" incorrectly.

U-boats reach the convoy areas more quickly, they could remain longer because of the fuel saved on the shorter journey. This change produced almost immediate results. Of the almost 600,000 tons of Allied shipping lost in June, about half was sunk by U-boats.

Dönitz, however, was still eager to put the wolf-pack strategy into effect. "I hoped to be able soon to fight a convoy battle," he recalled later; "that is, with a number of U-boats or U-boat groups. From an engagement of this nature, I confidently expected substantial results."

Dönitz therefore put out an order that every sighting of a convoy, no matter where the ships were, should be reported to headquarters by the U-boat commander. Once the report was received, any submarines near the reporting U-boat could be commanded to converge for the attack.

Since the fall of France, convoys had been following a route that took them north of Ireland. Dönitz therefore deployed his U-boats in the waters off the British Isles. The U-boats could be arranged in three basic formations: in a line moving back and forth to patrol a large patch of sea, or in a stationary line with the boats spaced about 25 miles apart, or in a large square-shaped formation, which varied in size according to the number of available U-boats and in which each boat was responsible for covering a given area.

When a convoy was spotted, a message was immediately dispatched to Dönitz' headquarters at Kerneval. Dönitz, who kept track of every U-boat, could then play a giant chess game, ordering nearby U-boats to the scene. He received valuable assistance from the cryptanalysis section of the German Navy, which was successfully deciphering British messages that spelled out convoy routes.

Acting on intercepted information, Dönitz made several attempts in the summer of 1940 to put the wolf-pack strategy into action, but each effort failed when the enemy changed course at the last moment. In September another convoy message was picked up, and Dönitz dispatched four submarines to attack. In spite of wretched weather, which hampered U-boat activity, five ships were sunk. Then, on the night of September 21, the wolf pack attacked a convoy of 41 ships, sinking 12.

On two successive nights in October, the 18th and the 19th, Dönitz' strategy achieved a double victory; wolf packs did such damage to two Allied convoys as to leave no doubt about the correctness of Dönitz' approach to submarine warfare. The exploit started in a manner reminiscent of Kretschmer's harrowing experience aboard the *U-99* in July. But this time the U-boat commander was able to summon a wolf pack to the scene.

The action began just before midnight on October 16, when Lieut. Commander Heinrich Bleichrodt in the *U-48* spotted from his conning tower a convoy about 180 miles northwest of the tiny island of Rockall. Creeping slowly toward him from the west were more than 30 small shadows. Three even smaller shadows were chasing up and down the flanks or across the front, like sheepdogs nudging forward a laggard and unwieldy flock.

Slowly and patiently in the darkness, Bleichrodt brought the surfaced *U-48* into position about a mile off the port

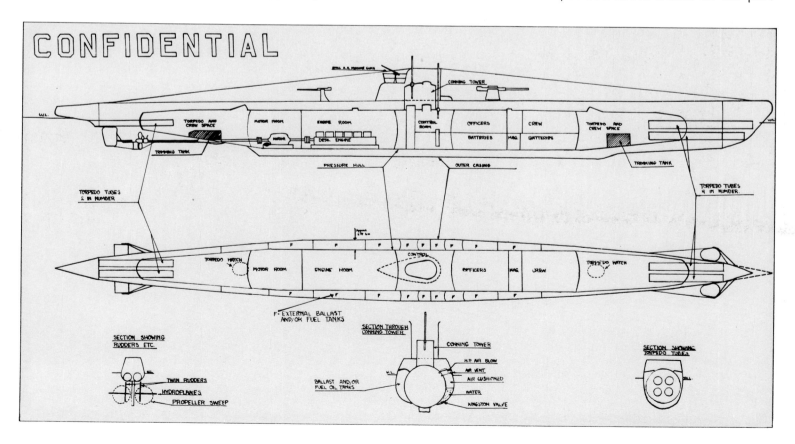

column of the convoy and remained there, watching the silhouettes slide across the moonlit southern sky. As soon as he could, he radioed Lorient the position, course, speed, number of ships and number of escorts in the convoy.

Bleichrodt now edged closer in toward the nearer column. Then, when the escorts were at their farthest point from him, he quickly went into the attack, firing a "fan" of three torpedoes toward a trio of ships that conveniently overlapped each other. Turning, he made off to the northwest, being careful not to go so fast that he might leave a telltale trail of white foam after him. At almost exactly 4 a.m., October 17, two dull explosions echoed across the water. Flames shot upward as the 10,000-ton French tanker *Languedoc* ignited, while the British merchantman *Scoresby* shuddered to a stop, her cargo of pit props—logs used to prevent coal mines from caving in—skidding across the decks and spilling in a wooden tide into the sea. Both of these ships went down.

A good start, Bleichrodt thought. But dawn was now at hand and he was forced to withdraw. He could shadow the convoy through the daylight hours, reporting all developments to Lorient at regular intervals. When night fell again,

THE TOP TEN U-BOAT ACES

These German U-boat commanders together sank a total of 318 ships during World War II, accounting for an astonishing 1,871,844 tons of Allied shipping. They are ranked here from left to right, according to amount of tonnage sunk.

Foremost among these aces was Otto Kretschmer. He attacked so relentlessly in the first year and a half of the War that he racked up the biggest tonnage total even though he was captured during an attack in the North Atlantic in March 1941 and spent the remaining four years in a prison camp.

Kretschmer's enthusiasm for submarine warfare was matched by that of Günther Prien, the dapper, quick-tempered hero of Scapa Flow and favorite of Admiral Dönitz and the German High Command. "I get more fun out of a really good convoy exercise than out of any leave," Prien once remarked.

The top 10 aces ranged all over the Atlantic. Wolfgang Lüth and Erich Topp scored heavily along the eastern coast of America, sometimes in sight of beach resorts. Heinrich Lehmann-Willenbrock, whose U-boat appears on the cover and on page 81, operated in the North Atlantic. Georg Lassen sank seven ships out of a convoy of 10 in a single night off the coast of South Africa, and Karl-Friedrich Merten daringly cruised underwater right into the harbor of Jamestown, St. Helena, in the South Atlantic, and sank a British tanker anchored there.

All but one of the aces survived the War. Prien was killed in the Atlantic in March 1942. Lüth came through the War unscathed, then was killed on shore in 1945, when he gave the wrong password and a German sentry shot him dead.

Otto Kretschmer
266,629 tons, 44 ships

Wolfgang Lüth
225,712 tons, 43 ships

Herbert Schultze
171,122 tons, 26 ships

Georg Lassen
167,601 tons, 28 ships

he planned to repeat his attack, perhaps in company with other U-boats now racing toward the area.

But shortly after daylight, at 7 a.m.—before he had a chance to take his boat down—he was startled by the cry "Aircraft ahead!" As he slammed the main hatch, a British Sunderland flying boat swooped down. He was still tightening the lock on the hatch, with the *U-48* already down to 60 feet and diving fast, when two bombs exploded close by. The vessel plunged on down with no lights, the crew clinging to whatever they could grasp, loose boxes and equipment crashing about, and Bleichrodt's own hands and arms numb

from the shock that had shuddered through the hatch.

Discipline quickly brought the *U-48* under control, but then came a sound every U-boat crew feared: propeller noises registered in the hydrophones. Bleichrodt knew that at least one of the escorts whose defenses he had so recently penetrated had received the Sunderland's report and was now above him, intent on revenge. As the asdic pings bounced off his hull, he went down to 600 feet and prepared to sit it out.

For eight hours, the depth charges exploded dully above him—none, fortunately, deeper than 400 feet—and all the

Erich Topp
193,684 tons, 34 ships

Karl-Friedrich Merten
186,064 tons, 29 ships

Victor Schütze
171,164 tons, 34 ships

Heinrich Lehmann-Willenbrock
166,596 tons, 22 ships

Heinrich Liebe
162,333 tons, 30 ships

Günther Prien
160,939 tons, 28 ships

time, as Bleichrodt realized bitterly, the convoy was escaping farther and farther eastward, undoubtedly upon a different course. Could there possibly now be enough U-boats disposed across the approaches to British home waters to cover every possible avenue of escape for the convoy?

That question and others were dominating the thoughts of the U-boat staff at Lorient, and those of Admiral Dönitz in particular. Where was the *U-48* now? Had Bleichrodt's disappearance robbed the U-boat service of an unprecedented opportunity?

The signal from the *U-48* had been clearly received and immediately acted upon, but a number of the U-boats directed toward the convoy still had many miles to cover before they would be in the area. Kretschmer, for instance, had already signaled that he would be at least an hour late at the rendezvous, and Heinrich Liebe in the *U-38* was apparently too far away to reach the concentration in time. For unless the convoy was caught within the next two days, it would reach safety. The only thing to do was to hope.

Luck was with the attackers. Liebe, patrolling by himself, spotted the convoy away to the south as dusk fell on October 17. He radioed Lorient, then stealthily approached the head of the port column and, around midnight, fired a fan of three torpedoes. Only one found its target, the freighter *Carsbreck,* whose timber cargo would keep her afloat until she reached port. Liebe then fired another fan half an hour later, and was mortified to realize, after too many seconds had passed, that all his torpedoes had missed.

But the most critical of his duties had been carried out: thanks to Liebe's radio message, Dönitz now knew exactly where Convoy SC-7 was—and, more important, where she would be when darkness came again. As a result, a "stripe" of submarines was formed across the convoy route. Fritz Frauenheim in the *U-101* sighted the starboard column leader early in the day, and by afternoon the pack was converging. In the 40 hours since Bleichrodt first spotted the convoy, it had traveled 250 miles to the southeast.

By now Kretschmer was on the scene in the *U-99,* intent upon demonstrating that convoys should be attacked from the middle, and that one torpedo was quite enough for one ship. Joachim Schepke in the *U-100,* Karl-Heinz Moehle in the *U-123* and Engelbert Endrass in the *U-46* were in position on the flanks, and Bleichrodt, who had been delayed

by the convoy escort's attack on the *U-48,* was now vainly racing to catch up from the rear.

At 8:15 p.m. Endrass fired the first torpedo and within 10 minutes the Swedish freighter *Convallaria* had capsized, her crew pulling away in two lifeboats, her buoyant pulpwood cargo keeping her upended for a quarter of an hour. Meantime the escorts were churning back and forth, failing to find the enemy in the blackness of the night, their asdic sets useless against surfaced U-boats. Next, Moehle in the *U-123* sank both the British freighter *Beatus,* which was loaded with timber and steel ingots, and the Dutch steamer *Boekolo,* which against all convoy orders had stopped to pick up survivors.

By now, the wolf pack was attacking the convoy with all its fury, and ships were going down everywhere. The British steamship *Creekirk* took her cargo of iron ore straight to the bottom. Shortly afterward the huge British steamship *Empire Miniver* lurched out of line, steam gushing from her decks as her crew piled into the boats and leaped from the decks. Then the Cardiff steamer *Fiscus* was blown to smithereens—one moment she was there, the next gone—leaving nothing but a huge billowing cloud above a whirlpool of debris.

Kretschmer was in the middle of the convoy, coolly picking off his targets. He had missed one ship on the convoy's flank, but hit another that went down in 20 seconds. Then he found a gap in the line and wheeled through it, shortly to find himself pursued by a huge British freighter, the *Assyrian,* which had spotted him in the moonlight. For 40 minutes he twisted and turned, avoiding the angle of the ship's stern gun; on the final twist he fired a torpedo that missed the *Assyrian* but hit another behind her, the British steamship *Empire Brigade.*

A night of chaos and confusion followed, filled with death and destruction for the unfortunate convoy—and high excitement and triumph for the U-boat crews. All around, ships were burning, blowing up, sinking. Some settled slowly and tiredly, the frigid waters lapping higher and higher until the final lurch. Others broke in half, with one section sticking upright out of the water until the imprisoned air leaked out and it went down with a rush and a gulp. The steamship *Sedgepool,* with her bow blown off, knifed down into the sea like a U-boat doing a crash dive, propellers still whirling high in the air.

Lit by explosions, burning wood and burning oil, debris littered the sea. Most of it was wood, for many of the cargoes were pit props. Broken wire lashings trailed menacingly in the water, tearing the flesh of desperate men who tried to climb on the oil-sodden timbers. Many of the struggling survivors were crushed or knocked unconscious as explosions churned the wooden maelstrom.

Of the 35 ships in Convoy SC-7, only 15 reached port. Besides the 18 accounted for by Bleichrodt and the wolf pack, two stragglers were picked off.

Seven U-boats had attacked the convoy, and none were lost. Kretschmer, Moehle and Frauenheim (the U-101 had finally dispatched the Assyrian) found when dawn broke that they had used all their torpedoes, and had to return to base for more. Kretschmer, it turned out, had sunk six ships and Moehle four, half of SC-7's total losses.

As Kretschmer, Moehle and Frauenheim were leaving the scene of carnage, word came from Lorient that a fast convoy of 49 vessels, including many tankers, was approaching on almost the same course as SC-7. The U-boats that had torpedoes left were joined by Liebe in the U-38 and Prien in the U-47. The violent pattern of the previous night was repeated some 200 miles westward—but this time, the heat and fury were more intense and the human casualties greater, for oil burns more fiercely than wood. Twelve ships went to the bottom before dawn brought relief to Convoy HX-79 and enabled the tired escort crews to count the losses and make a last sweep of the littered water in an attempt to save a few more men.

The U-boat crews were tired too, but with the difference that victory brings. Buoyed by triumph, they may have been a bit puzzled by their successes. They were fighting the British at sea. Whatever the Führer might say about the decadence of the British, the men were aware of the naval tradition that imbued the enemy. Many recalled Britain's unequaled reputation for losing battles but winning wars. Would the tide someday turn? For the moment, they were too exhilarated by their victory to really care. They found triumphal welcomes waiting for them all, congratulations from Dönitz, exhortations from the Führer himself to do even better and ecstatic encomiums on their exploits broadcast over the German radio by Germany's propaganda chief, Dr. Joseph Goebbels.

The wolf-pack victories in September and October were followed by a brief letup in submarine warfare. After the extended operations, it was necessary to rest and refit the submarines and their crews. Moreover, as November came on, the weather began to deteriorate. Heinz Schaeffer, a U-boat commander, described with particular intensity the ordeal to which winter put U-boat commanders and crews.

"For four weeks the wind had been howling from every quarter at 55 to 60 miles an hour, with heavy rain and the thermometer only a few degrees above zero. I was up on the bridge. There was of course no protection there, just the icy steel bulkheads, so it was impossible to work up any warmth. Lashed to the rail as I was, the leather safety-belt reinforced with steel bit deep into my ribs. It had been known for the watch on the bridge to be washed overboard in heavy seas—in one boat the relief had gone up to take over and just found no one there. The force of the seas breaking over us now was terrific.

"The officer of the watch had warned the look-out aft of a big wave ahead. Ducking, we groped for something to hold on to and waited for it. It was indescribable. Everything went green as tons of sea water poured over us, ears, nostrils and mouths choked and eyes blinded and stinging. Waterproof clothing, sea boots and jackets weren't much use, for in spite of tying up every opening the ice-cold water still soaked in. My hands were stiff with cold, but I still had to keep my binoculars before my eyes, since it was a point of honor to let nothing escape us—we simply had to keep keyed up on the look-out for ship or plane."

The winter of 1940-1941 in the North Atlantic was one of the worst in memory. U-boat operations were sharply curtailed and, accordingly, Allied shipping losses dropped off. Meanwhile the British were busy attempting to improve their defenses against U-boats, and Dönitz and his aces were girding for a renewal of the wolf-pack attacks. In the spring, shipping losses would mount again as the wolf packs stalked the convoy routes. Another year would pass before Dönitz would have a U-boat force of the size he had been pleading for. But the strategy for waging the most devastating kind of submarine warfare had already been found.

A SUBMARINER'S EERIE WORLD

STRESS AND MISERY BENEATH THE SEA

Germans regarded their sea wolves as heroes who led glamorous lives, but the reality of life on a U-boat was something else again. Submariners lived in a tight, fetid world, and their life was a mixture of boredom, discomfort and terror as is shown in these unusual pictures. Many were taken by Lothar-Günther Buchheim, a German photographer who accompanied the *U-96* on a mission. Crews occupied quarters jammed with engines, instruments or torpedoes, sleeping on planking above the missiles until these had been spent on targets, leaving room for bunks and hammocks.

The diesels raised temperatures to as high as 120° F. Air became suffocatingly stale during long periods underwater. Fresh water was scarce; there were no showers and nobody bathed for up to three months on patrol. The odor of hardworking bodies was added to the smell of bilges, toilets, cooking, mildewed clothes, diesel fuel and the lemon cologne the men used to rub the salt from their faces.

There was no privacy or quiet. Always in the background were burning lights, the squall of radio communications, the squish of wet gum boots, the whir of a bilge pump, the sucking of air-intake valves and the throbbing of diesels.

Danger was always present. In heavy weather, the ocean coursed over the conning tower in solid green walls, sometimes washing men overboard. In October 1941, as the *U-106* crossed the Bay of Biscay on a calm blue day, a new watch climbed topside to find that the entire four-man shift they were to replace had disappeared. A freak wave from the stern had swept them away.

Such ominous incidents added to the U-boat paranoia the Germans called *Blechkoller*, or tin-can neurosis, a form of nervous strain that could drive them to violent hysteria particularly under depth-charge attack. When Allied subchasers gave up an attack, the commander's first thought was to bring his boat gasping to the surface. The panic among the crew had to be calmed immediately through the leadership, experience and cool-headedness of the skipper. With luck, he would soon find a kill, and the victory would further alleviate the crew's tension.

In a choppy sea, a crew member clings to a cable while gingerly working his way back to the conning tower after making repairs on the stern.

A steersman in a surfaced U-boat, guiding his sub on orders from the bridge, is drenched through the open hatch by waves breaking on deck

Crewmen resting in their bunks in the U-boat's torpedo compartment are surrounded by newly laid-in provisions—potatoes, hams, smoked bacon, sausages, bread—as every inch of space is utilized. But after three weeks, the black bread always turned so hoary with mold that the crews called the loaves "white rabbits," and ate only the insides.

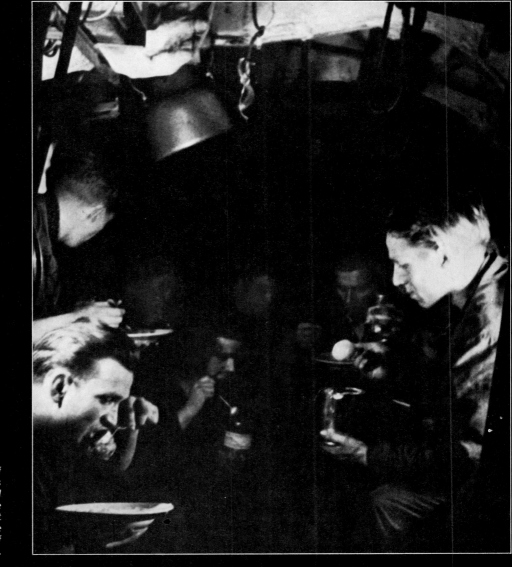

Squatting on their bunks, torpedomen wolf down boiled meat and potatoes. Food was devoured in a hurry so that men on duty could be relieved and fed without requiring the cook to prepare separate meals for different shifts. Although conditions were crude, the submarine service was given the best rations of any branch of Germany's armed forces.

Working and sleeping in shifts around the clock, torpedomen make the best of their cramped quarters. They developed the ability to sleep through any noise short of depth charges. Those on duty—like the men adjusting the guidance mechanism of a torpedo at center—would eat when finished working, then take over the narrow bunks behind them.

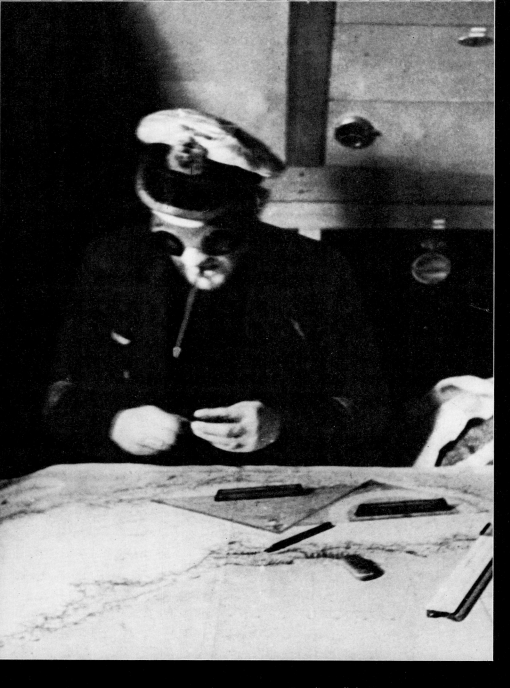

Prowling off the European coast at night, a
submarine commander studies a message
from U-boat Command in France, then
pinpoints on a chart the location of an Allied
convoy bound for the Mediterranean. While
plotting its course, he wears red glasses so
his eyes will not have to adjust to the dark when
he climbs to the bridge to direct the attack.

Torpedomen check the guidance systems on
their torpedoes during a patrol. The missiles
required constant attention: batteries needed
recharging, the guidance system called for
constant adjustments, propellants and firing
mechanisms had to be checked. Despite
these efforts, many torpedoes malfunctioned or
missed their targets by going astray.

A periscope view of Allied ships moments
before a U-boat attack demonstrates the
vulnerability of unsuspecting surface vessels to
subs lying in wait just below the waves. A
favorite tactic of U-boat captains was to race
their surfaced vessels ahead of a convoy,
then submerge in its path and wait for the ship
to sail into the cross hairs of the periscope.

With his cap reversed to keep the peak from
obstructing his view, U-boat commander
Kurt Diggins studies a convoy through the
periscope. His gloved left hand turns the
instrument while his right adjusts the eyepiece
which is cushioned with foam rubber. In the
tension of an attack, U-boat skippers would
sometimes dig out chunks of the foam.

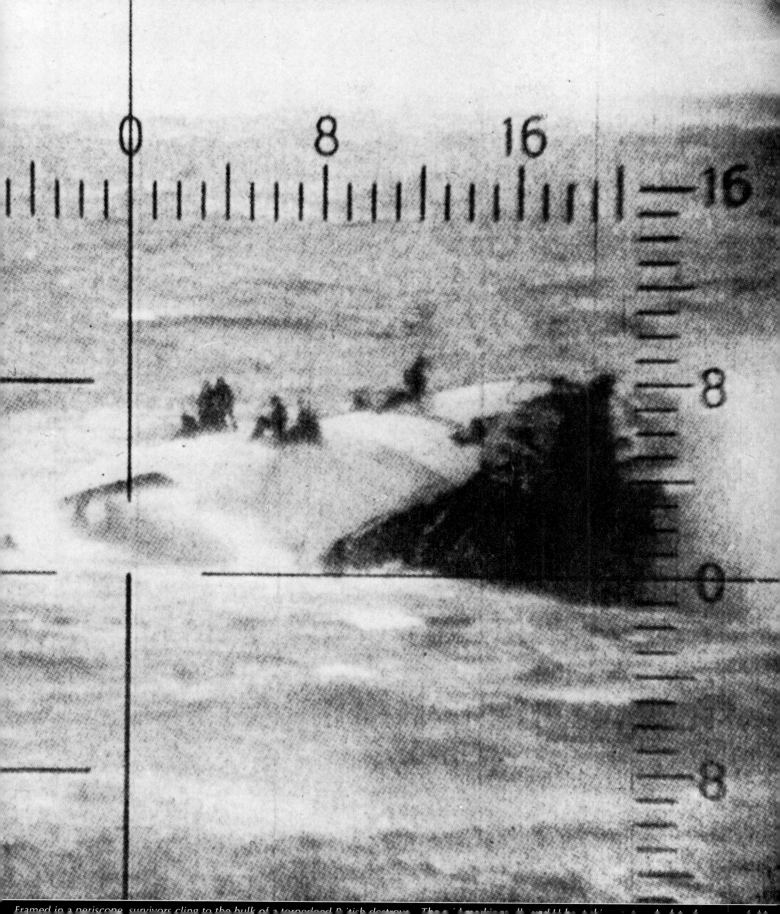

Framed in a periscope, survivors cling to the hulk of a torpedoed British destroyer. These submarine-launched U-boat victims

A hydrophone man listens to the propellers of approaching destroyers.

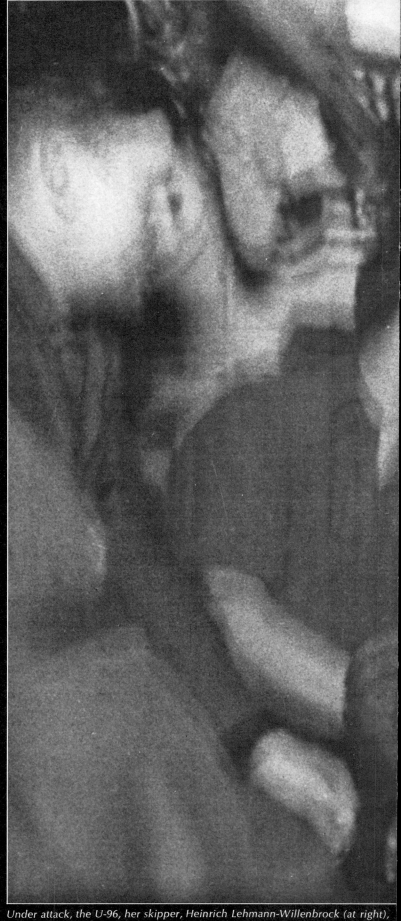

Under attack, the U-96, her skipper, Heinrich Lehmann-Willenbrock (at right),

A member of the crew peers into the below-decks gloom in a far death dive. The submarine's commander was one of Germany's top U-boat ace

Celebrating a successful patrol, a submarine crew joins in singing beer-hall songs with accordion accompaniment and plenty of lager. Once their torpedoes

were used up, the U-boat men could expect a week or more of shore leave.

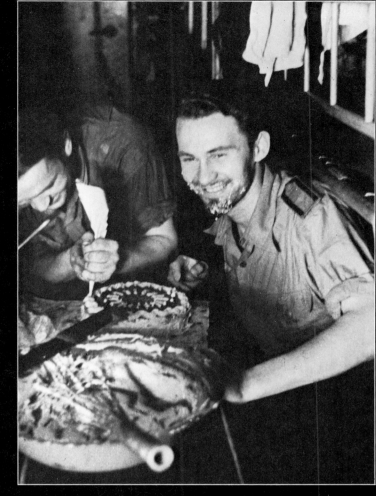

In a lull during a patrol in the Atlantic, submariners take time out to decorate a cake and sample its icing. The cake was baked in the sub's cramped galley for a celebration of an officer's birthday.

Bound for home, a U-boat crew paints pennants with the tonnage of Allied ships they sank during the patrol. The flags were flown from the conning tower as the sub entered port, to cheers from waiting comrades.

THE SINKING OF A U-BOAT

Exploding depth charges produce a mountainous geyser from the deep as the U.S. Coast Guard cutter Spencer attacks the German submarine U-175.

A BRIEF RISE BEFORE THE FINAL PLUNGE

The terror that U-boats spread was matched by the terror that the men on the U-boats faced. For being a U-boat captain or crew member was one of World War II's most hazardous occupations. Statistics tell the grim story. Germany lost 28,542 of its 41,300 submariners, and 753 of its 863 operational U-boats. The sinking of one of those boats by Allied vessels is recorded in the dramatic pictures on these pages, from the moment the depth charges were dropped until the crew of the fatally damaged U-boat surrendered and was marched off to a prisoner-of-war camp.

The episode began when Captain Gerhardt Muntz, while searching from his conning tower for Allied ships in the North Atlantic 600 miles west of England, spotted an approaching convoy. At the same time, Muntz's submarine, the *U-175*, was herself seen by the U.S. Coast Guard cutter *Spencer* in the vanguard of the convoy. Hastily, the *U-175* dived, and for a short time successfully evaded detection. But trailing the *Spencer* in 11 parallel columns were the 19 tankers and 38 freighters of Convoy HX-233, an irresistible target. Muntz decided to chance an attack. It was a fateful decision. As the *U-175* eased up from the ocean depths, the *Spencer* passed right over her, and the cutter's sonar detection device picked up the sub.

Commander Harold S. Berdine, aboard the *Spencer*, ordered an immediate depth-charge barrage: 11 of the lethal drums, set to explode underwater at 50 and 100 feet. Then, anxious to neutralize the sub before the convoy arrived, Berdine released 11 more depth charges. The furious assault worked: the *U-175*'s air pumps and diving controls were damaged, and Muntz had no choice but to bring his crippled submarine to the surface.

As the *U-175*'s conning tower rose into view a mile and a half behind the cutter, the convoy ships and the *Spencer*'s sister cutter, the *Duane*, opened fire. It was all over in moments. Captain Muntz and six of his crew died on the *U-175*'s deck. The remaining crew members jumped overboard; while they were still bobbing in the seas, the *U-175* sank to the bottom.

A submariner calls out for assistance from the Spencer moments after the U-175 sank. Calm, warm (54° F.) seas made rescue work less hazardous.

The badly damaged U-175 surfaces and is immediately caught in a fusillade of artillery and machine-gun fire as the cutter Spencer closes in for the kill.

The U-175 goes down stern first as officers and men from the Spencer, who had boarded the sub for a quick inspection, watch from a lifeboat nearby.

Saved from drowning, a submariner from the U-175 grabs a boarding net on the cutter Duane. Dangling near his cheek is his life-jacket mouthpiece.

A dazed U-boat survivor is led off by two of the Spencer's crewmen. Commander Berdine of the cutter later reported some of the survivors as "hysterical" during the rescue operation.

Resentful German submariners are ordered to peel off their clothing while being searched aboard the Duane. The captured men told the cutter's officers that the first salvo of depth charges from the Spencer cracked the sub's hull, jammed her forward steering mechanism and broke her air pump system.

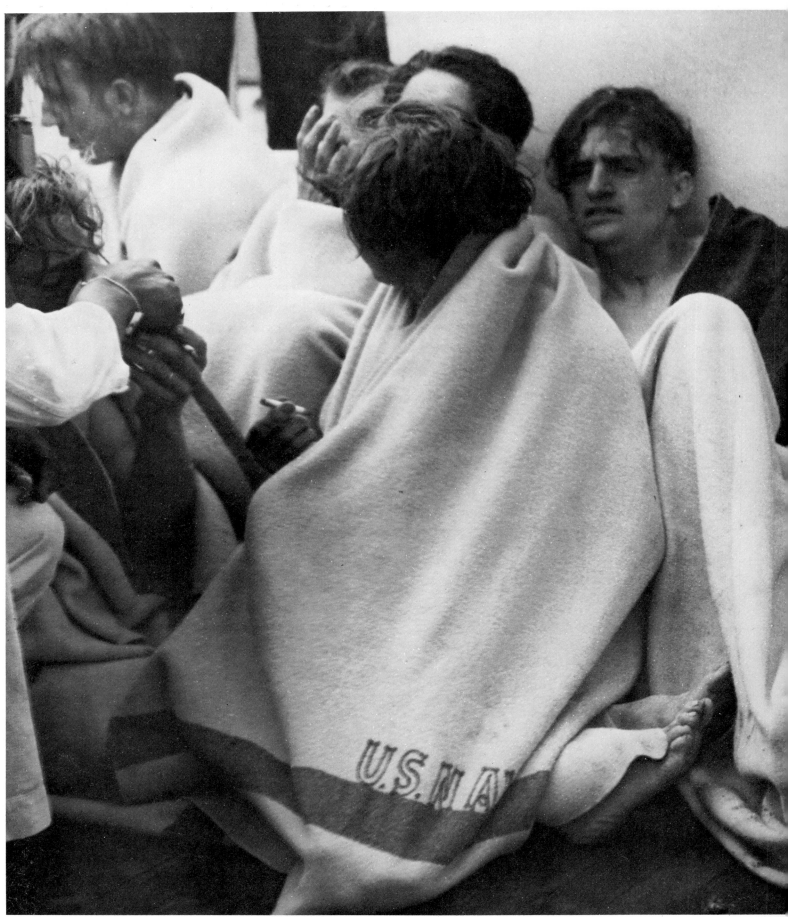

Swathed in blankets and showing stress, the U-175's survivors huddle on the Spencer's quarterdeck. Taken below, they were dressed in borrowed denims and fed

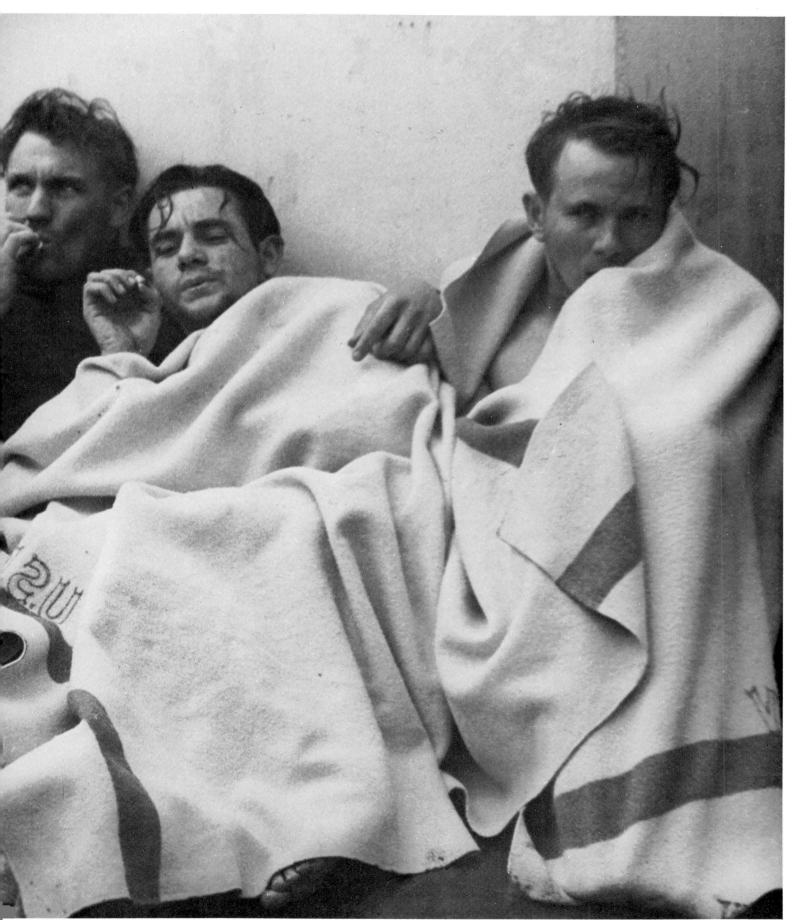

a meal of corned beef and potatoes. The Spencer rescued 19 members of the U-175's crew. Twenty-two more German sailors were saved by the cutter Duane.

Triumphant members of the *Spencer's* crew line the rail in front of a Popeye cartoon painted on the funnel to celebrate their victory over the *U-175*. It was the second kill for the ship.

Commander Harold S. Berdine (front right) and his fellow officers celebrate the sinking of the German submarine at a victory dinner in the flag-decorated wardroom of the *Spencer.*

British Marines march off the German prisoners of war from the U-175 at Gourock, an Allied naval base at the mouth of the River Clyde in Scotland. From there they were taken by transport to a prisoner-of-war camp. The Spencer and Duane are docked behind the prisoners.

4

For the weekend sailors who so gallantly responded to the advertisement in the London *Times* suggesting that "gentlemen with yachting experience" apply for commissions in the Royal Navy Volunteer Reserve, there was a sudden and rude awakening when they found themselves aboard the escort vessels that accompanied the first convoys. In place of white sails were guns and depth charges; in place of beautiful girls were tired, grim-featured and often acid-tongued commanding officers, who were trying to carry out a difficult job that was made even more difficult by inadequate equipment, poor supplies, and a lack of planning and coordination between ships with similar responsibilities. It was a long time before things got better; before that, they got much worse.

The hard-bitten merchant captains who sailed in the first convoys had a similar experience. The convoys were badly organized, makeshift collections of 30 to 45 freighters and tankers that were attempting the novel experience of sailing 3,500 miles together in close formation. A large number of the ships were so decrepit and unseaworthy that only the urgent demands of wartime made it at all possible to justify their use.

The conditions of the ships and the inexperience of their crew members made the duty of the escort vessels an especially onerous one: they had to accompany these motley armadas, shepherd them through dangerous waters, protect them from submarine attack and bring them safely to port. The task was awesome; yet the very outcome of the War depended upon its being carried out successfully. It would have been a challenge to the most grizzled of seamen, but at the beginning of the War, the Royal Navy had had no other choice than to man the escort vessels with any able-bodied recruits it could find—weekend sailors and even those who were without any previous seagoing experience at all. The adventures of a little corvette called the *Bluebell* were typical.

Commander Robert Evan Sherwood first took the *Bluebell* to sea in the summer of 1940. It quickly became apparent to him that "only three or four of the crew of 52 were capable of any real action of any kind at all." Of his three officers, two were Canadians. "They were fine chaps, but they had had very little training. One was a lawyer and the other was in the leather business. One of them was very

VITAL ARMADAS

pale but went green when he was seasick, which sometimes lasted for two days. Once I was in my cabin and the ship was not quite doing what she should be doing, so I asked: 'How is your head?' I wanted to know where we were going, for on a ship 'head' means 'course.' He answered, 'Much better, thank you, sir.' "

Sherwood counted himself fortunate to have gained his experience on small ships, because corvettes, "though fine ships, are not the easiest." The *Bluebell* seemed to be always wallowing, always fighting the sea. She "would do everything except turn over," Sherwood noted. "In bad weather the cook couldn't control the galley to give everyone proper food—not that there was much desire to eat. It is one thing to be able to do something on land or in good conditions and another to be able to do it in bad conditions when you are seasick. Then you have to be able to do it in your sleep."

In October, the *Bluebell* got its first big taste of battle as one of the escort ships accompanying Convoy SC-7, the ill-fated convoy that was first spotted by Heinrich Bleichrodt in the *U-48* on October 16. The convoy consisted of 35 elderly, lumbering vessels that were on their way to Great Britain from Nova Scotia.

Typically, the escort for SC-7 had been flung together in a hurry. In addition to the *Bluebell,* there were two sloops. The commanders of these vessels had never met before, and there was almost no coordination among them, although they had been forewarned by the Admiralty that there were U-boats in the area in which they were traveling. A predawn attack by Bleichrodt was their first intimation that trouble was at hand: two ships were sunk. One of the escort vessels fruitlessly depth-charged the suspected point of attack and the convoy pushed on. Then, the following night, the U-boat pack struck en masse. Suddenly there was a tremendous flash—another one of the SC-7's ships had been hit. "I was on the bridge," recalled Sherwood; "it was around 8:15 p.m. I went in towards the convoy to see if I could get any information." He searched the area where he thought the explosion had taken place, but could determine nothing, in part because the escort ships had established no organized procedure for communicating information to one another during an attack. "I had never seen the *Fowey,* one of the sloops, before and she had never seen me. We

each did what we thought best at that particular moment."

The wolf-pack onslaught created total havoc. "Suddenly it was 'bang, bang, bang!' and the place was lit up like Piccadilly Circus." A total of 16 ships went down; one was sunk when she stopped to pick up survivors. At the height of the disaster, Sherwood again moved in to see what was happening. None of the escort vessels had ever experienced a pack attack before, and no one could understand how a single U-boat could inflict so much damage. To add to the confusion, someone suddenly opened fire on the *Bluebell*. Whether it was a submarine or a merchant ship, Sherwood did not wait to see. He put another ship between the *Bluebell* and the line of fire, knowing that in the heat of battle a corvette could be mistaken for a submarine by a merchantman.

The confusion quickly turned into a nightmare. "We were fumbling around in the dark," Sherwood reported. "There were survivors all over the place. The attack went on until one or two in the morning. I never saw an escort that night. And I didn't drop a single depth charge and I don't think anyone else did."

In fact, the only useful service that the escort vessels performed after the wolf pack had struck was to pick up survivors. Sherwood alone took on board 308 men.

The following night a similar calamity befell the 49 ships constituting Convoy HX-79 and its escort. Faster than SC-7, HX-79 also had much more formidable protection. Two destroyers, a minesweeper, four new corvettes and three asdic-fitted trawlers formed a protective screen around the convoy. Yet HX-79 lost 12 ships without being able to inflict the slightest damage in return—once again as the result of a wolf-pack attack.

The experience of Lieut. Commander G. T. Cooper, in charge of one of the destroyers, the *Sturdy,* sounds much like Sherwood's. Cooper and his crew had had only one previous turn at escort work in submarine areas, and that had proved to be uneventful. "I had no details of this convoy, nor did I know the nature of the escort and I had never met any of the Commanding Officers of the other ships. No plan of action in the event of attack had therefore been discussed between us."

When the attack developed, each ship took individual action as fresh emergencies arose. The flanks of the convoy went unprotected for long periods of time, while the escort vessels violated one of the first principles of effective convoy discipline by running off from the ships to follow up elusive contacts with the enemy or to pick up survivors. As the night wore on, the convoy and its escorts found themselves strung out along an ever-thinning line. All told, HX-79 lost almost one quarter of its total force, and this despite its traveling with an escort that was numerically strong enough to provide it with ample protection.

In just two nights, 28 merchant ships had been destroyed by the wolf packs, and every one of the attacking U-boats had escaped unscathed.

So ineffectual did escorts appear in the face of wolf-pack attack that men at all levels of command began to wonder whether it made any sense to bunch ships together to form huge targets for the enemy to strike at will.

The problem was twofold: a lack of discipline and a chronic shortage of escort craft. The shortage had been accentuated by shipping losses suffered in the spring and summer of 1940 in the fall of Norway and France. The subsequent establishment of German submarine bases in France made it impossible for British ships to use their own Channel ports—primarily Southampton, Plymouth and Portsmouth—and effectively closed off access to Great Britain from the southwest. In the entire area of what the British called the Western Approaches, the only access remaining from the west was the route around Northern Ireland, through the North Channel and across the Irish Sea to Britain's west-coast ports, Liverpool and Glasgow.

Since even the doubters could find no substitute for the convoy system, the convoys went on. Assembling one and shepherding it across the sea involved a host of enormously complex problems. The difficulties began to assert themselves from the moment the ships came together at their initial rendezvous point—more often than not, outside the Nova Scotia ports of Halifax or Sydney if eastbound, and outside Liverpool or Glasgow if westbound. Freighters large and small joined with tankers old and new, perhaps a passenger ship or two, sometimes a merchantman converted for heavy cargo such as tanks, trucks or landing craft.

Unequal in size, these ships differed as well in their maneuverability, their mechanical condition, their speed, their capacity for maintaining their positions, their signaling and other equipment, the caliber of their crews, even the ability of the men to make out orders shouted from the bridge—which might be manned by Dutchmen or Poles, Norwegians or Danes, Belgians or French Canadians. And even when English was the common language aboard ship, a Scotsman did not always find it easy to understand his mate from Southampton, and vice versa.

Once a convoy was under way, it would form into a wide rectangle of eight to 12 short columns, with 1,000 yards between columns and from 400 to 600 yards between the stern of each ship and the bow of the one following (pages 126-127). A 40-ship convoy (30 to 45 merchant ships constituted the average aggregation for the first three years of the War) would be arranged in eight columns five ships deep, covering an area almost four miles across by about two miles deep. Only four or five escorts could be spared by the Navy from duty elsewhere to guard the perimeter. And in charge of this tiny force would be the command ship, usually an old World War I destroyer, placed ahead of the formation, or at a point from which—depending on weather conditions or perhaps the position of the moon—an attack might come.

Difficult as it was to keep the armada operating as a unit, there was an additional complication in the matter of command. The escort commander was responsible not only for the conduct of the escort ships, but for the entire convoy. On his shoulders fell the job of directing changes in course and issuing whatever other instructions were necessary for the safety of all the ships. The convoy commodore, from his flagship among the merchant ships, was responsible for maintaining the internal discipline of the convoy proper, in terms of navigation and holding to position.

Unfortunately, there were times when the duties and responsibilities of escort commander and convoy commodore overlapped. This caused a certain awkwardness, especially when the escort commander, usually a commander or lieutenant-commander in the Royal Navy or the Royal Canadian Navy, was considerably junior to the convoy commodore, who was likely to be a retired rear-admiral or vice-admiral with the acting rank of commodore, Royal Naval Reserve. It took more than a little mutual tact and courtesy for an admiral to accept orders given to him by a youthful lieutenant-commander. Whatever friction developed was generally minor and short-lived. Both officers understood the necessity for cooperation.

Once the armada was in formation, it had to be guided round the clock by the escorts across a sea that could be glassy one day, turbulent the next. The ships had to keep station, that is, they had to stay in their proper positions in the convoy, and make as little smoke as possible in order to avoid attracting a sub. When laden with their precious cargoes, they wallowed sluggishly into the danger areas of the eastern leg of the voyage near the northwest Irish coast, where the U-boats waited. When empty and riding high on the return voyage, the convoy ships might have to butt their way into howling gales in order to reach the refuge of North American ports.

Through it all, the escorts acted as watchdogs, chivying the laggards into place, scurrying about with instructions to close up, ease out, make less smoke, or tighten the blackout at night. There was another problem: occasionally a merchantman disobeyed sailing instructions and left oil trails, dumped garbage and pumped bilges in daylight—telltale signs for the enemy to spot.

Even when all was going well, there was the continual shield for the escorts to provide: the constant weaving back and forth across the front of the formation with asdic directed ahead to pick up submerged foe lying in wait; out and in again along each flank, watching for attackers sneaking in as dusk fell; the constant patrolling astern, always on guard against the surfaced U-boat, whose commander knew quite well that only one escort ship, or two at most, could be spared to crisscross the wide tail of the convoy—and that four to six miles was a wide stretch for just one or two escorts to cover.

At any moment, there might come a warning of danger ahead: a signal flashed to indicate a sighting. And the whole plodding mass of shipping had to be turned in concert to dodge the threat, often making so sudden and sharp a curve that the ships on the inside of the turn were crowded dangerously close together while those on the outside became so widely separated as to risk losing contact with one another. Now the commanders of the escort ships needed all their skill, their foresight and their patience—and all the speed that could be coaxed from their overworked engines. Inside the convoy, the commodore worried about the dangers of collision as the ships turned simultaneously to their new course away from the threatening U-boat. And when it was all done and the convoy was safely on its new course with the danger point well astern, the whole maneuver had to be repeated in the reverse direction to get the convoy back on its original course.

Often the U-boats would not be detected in time for either evasive or offensive action to be taken. Sometimes, as at night, the danger was not apparent until the enemy had

Bobbing like corks and every bit as seaworthy, corvettes like the one at left above were the ideal convoy escorts, inexpensively produced and able to survive and maneuver in the worst kind of weather. But the 1,010-ton vessels were notoriously uncomfortable. Because of their broad beams and rounded bottoms, they rolled viciously, tossing sailors out of their bunks and making even the hardiest skippers queasy.

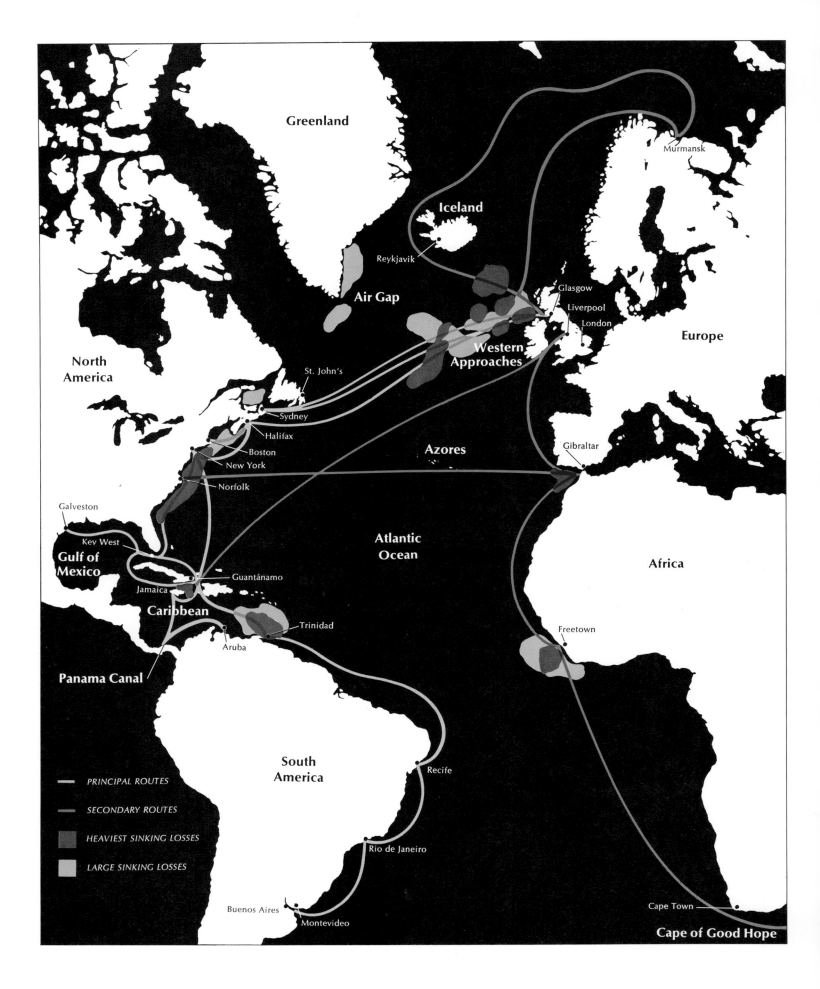

Greenland

Iceland

Reykjavik

Air Gap

Murmansk

North
America

St. John's

Sydney

Halifax

Boston

New York

Norfolk

Glasgow
Liverpool
London

Western
Approaches

Europe

Azores

Gibraltar

Galveston

Key West

Gulf of
Mexico

Jamaica

Guantánamo

Caribbean

Aruba

Trinidad

Atlantic
Ocean

Africa

Freetown

Panama Canal

South
America

Recife

Rio de Janeiro

Buenos Aires

Montevideo

Cape Town

Cape of Good Hope

PRINCIPAL ROUTES

SECONDARY ROUTES

HEAVIEST SINKING LOSSES

LARGE SINKING LOSSES

sliced deep into the heart of the convoy. When the attack came, there was the blinding glare of explosions, the frantic search for the enemy and the heart-chilling sight of a sea aflame with burning oil or dotted with timbers, furniture, upturned boats and dead or dying men.

The Happy Time of the U-boats—that period early in the War when things were going so well for the German subs—was, not surprisingly, a time of nightmare for the convoys. Try though they did, the escorts were incapable of protecting their charges effectively. For one thing, the Admiralty had been slow to recognize that U-boats did not have to be submerged to attack convoys; too much reliance had thus been placed on asdic, which was effective only when the vessels were submerged. For another, it was hoped that if the attacks were launched on the surface, the lookouts would spot the U-boats. How the lookouts were supposed to do this on gray days or dark nights was a question never considered at top level. Moreover, the lookouts were for the most part without real experience. They stood for hours on end crouched against the fury of a malignant wind that burned their faces and brought tears to their stinging eyes. When they tried inexpertly to use their binoculars, spray fogged the lenses and occasionally froze on them. And as they scanned the sea from their lookout posts, they found the low, gray silhouettes of trimmed-down U-boats virtually invisible even in fair light.

Haggard and red-eyed, the officers aboard the escort ships drove themselves to the very limits of their endurance—four hours on, four hours off, day after day until the end of the voyage. Years later, Nicholas Monsarrat, author of *The Cruel Sea,* wrote in another book about those grinding, tortured days:

"Strain and tiredness at sea induce a sort of hypnosis: you seem to be moving in a bad dream, pursued not by terrors but by an intolerable routine. You come off watch at midnight, soaked, twitching, your eyes raw with the wind and staring at shadows; you brew a cup of tea in the wardroom pantry and strip off the top layer of sodden clothes; you do, say, an hour's intricate cyphering, and thereafter snatch a few hours' sleep between wet blankets. . . . Every night for seventeen nights on end, you're woken up at ten to four by the bosun's mate, and you stare at the deckhead and think;

My God, I *can't* go up there again in the dark and filthy rain, and stand another four hours of it. But you can, of course; it becomes automatic in the end."

As much a part of watch duty as scouring the seas for U-boats was keeping visual contact with the rest of the ships in the convoy. Throughout the night, the watch officer hung grimly on to the vague, lurching shadow of the nearest ship, praying that she would still be there when the next flurry of rain or snow had cleared or when the next routine zig-zag was completed.

Often, when dawn filtered through the shrouded sky, the watch would find that the ship indeed was there—the only one in sight: both ships had lost station in the night. Anxious watchers on both ships would then scan a horizon bare of the rest of the convoy. Two ships sailing alone were exactly what U-boat commanders were seeking. Where was the rest of the convoy—ahead or astern? If ahead, could the strays possibly catch up? If astern, how long should they wait? Ahead or astern, had the convoy changed course during the night, and was it now following a divergent track?

Early in the War, strayed ships had no way of making contact with the body of the convoy. There was no radar (it would not come into use at sea until the spring of 1941), and ship-to-ship communication had to be conducted by means of flags, signal lamps or electric bullhorns. Radio silence was maintained, and radio could be used only for receiving coded instructions from the Admiralty—but not for acknowledging them. Even if a strayed ship were to broadcast an appeal for help, it would not be answered by the ships in the convoy, for no convoy would dare break radio silence—and risk having a U-boat pick up the broadcast—for the sake of a straggler or two. Nor were stragglers always welcome back, for there was always the danger that a U-boat, instead of attacking the lone ship, might trail her in hopes of being led to the convoy.

Yet another flaw in the early convoy system was the inability of the escorts to complete the Atlantic crossing. This was owing not so much to the difficulty of refueling them, though that was a factor, as to the continuing shortage of the necessary vessels. They could go only so far before they were needed for another convoy. For the westbound convoys, "so far," as determined by the Admiralty, was, until July 1940, 15° W. (about 200 miles west of Ireland).

The Battle of the Atlantic centered around the shipping routes shown here. Areas where the greatest numbers of ships were sunk are indicated in red, with the heaviest losses in deep red. The U-boats began their attacks in the Western Approaches, near Britain, and later divided their effort between the Greenland area and the coast of Africa. Next the East Coast of the United States became the main target region. Then the subs moved down to the Caribbean, before returning to the area west of Britain.

The theory—and indeed the fact—was that the area of maximum danger was in the Western Approaches, and it was there that the merchantmen would be in greatest need of escort protection. But as the U-boats became bolder, and especially after the French bases extended their range farther and farther into the Atlantic, the limits of escort had to be stretched: to 17° W. until October 1940, then to 19° W. until April 1941, when it was extended to 35° W.—more than halfway across the ocean.

When a westbound convoy reached the point where the Royal Navy escort could go no farther, the convoy dispersed and the ships sailed on independently to their destinations. The escort, meanwhile, was making rendezvous with an eastbound convoy that had started out with a local Royal Canadian Navy escort and had continued on as a group by itself, though sometimes with an armed merchant cruiser.

The rendezvous between the British naval escort and the eastbound convoy was difficult and nerve-racking. Navigational problems caused by dirty weather or U-boat attack often delayed and sometimes prevented the meeting; but there was no other way to give the convoys any degree of cross-Atlantic protection.

A shortage of trained men and experienced officers, a scarcity of escort ships and up-to-date equipment, a lack of understanding of the problems of convoy protection in the face of the new, expertly coordinated and ruthlessly delivered U-boat attacks—all continued to conspire against the convoy system. Its detractors went on damning it, with some cause, as inadequate and ineffectual, and some urged its discontinuance.

Yet it was the strategy of convoy—once all the mistakes had been learned and corrected—that would prove to be the most effective way of reducing the menace of the submarines. Throughout the War, ships sailing unescorted were hunted and destroyed at about four times the rate of ships traveling in convoy. In the end it was the solution of the problem of how to protect convoys that swung the Battle of the Atlantic in the Allies' favor.

Changes, almost imperceptible to the combatants on both sides, had already started taking place by the time the Germans launched their ferocious wolf-pack raids. In July of 1940, a new sea training base, known as the H.M.S. *Western Isles,* was established at Tobermory on the Hebridean island of Mull. Here, officers and men of every newly commissioned escort vessel were put through a month's intensive training in seamanship and antisubmarine warfare, aboard their ships but under the penetrating scrutiny of Commodore (Vice-Admiral, retired) Gilbert O. Stephenson, variously known as "Monkey," the "Terror of Tobermory," or "Lord of the *Western Isles.*"

It was sometimes claimed by members of his family or by old shipmates that a normal human heart did beat somewhere behind the commodore's impressive array of ribbons, but if so, his humanity was carefully concealed from those undergoing his training program.

Lieut. Commander D. A. Rayner, R.N.V.R., who had just taken command of one of the first ocean-going corvettes, the H.M.S. *Verbena,* remembered how "we were beaten into bruised efficiency. At any time of the day or night the lash might fall. 'Send away a boat! Let go a second anchor! Rig sheer-legs and hoist your boat clear of the water! Prepare to tow forward! Prepare to take a merchant-ship in tow! Send a boarding party to *Western Isles!* Your ship is dragging her anchor, weigh and proceed!' At first we squealed as we leapt. Later we learned to achieve the leap without the squeal."

Sometimes Stephenson sent the ships out to sea on training exercises separately, sometimes in company with other corvettes or sloops, sometimes with the base submarine, to train the asdic operators. But whether alone or in groups, whether at night or in daytime, whether in fair weather or foul, all trainee crews could be quite certain that the commodore's fertile imagination would produce some extraordinary complication to add to the already arduous program. Mock fires would have to be put out just when the asdic contacts were most promising; imaginary surface raiders would be conjured up in the middle of a fueling-at-sea exercise; or, with half of the members of the crew ashore attending a lecture, the ship would all of a sudden be ordered away to put a landing party on a remote beach—where, inevitably, the men would find the commodore himself waiting, watching their fumbling and exhausted efforts with a bleak, disparaging eye.

There were occasional moments of something approaching comic relief. According to Rear-Admiral W. S. Chalmers, who served in the Admiralty and used yet another of the commodore's nicknames when writing about him, "'Puggy' Stephenson believed in keeping the new ships' companies 'on their toes,' and would pay them surprise visits to test their readiness. On one occasion he crept up the side of a frigate and when he alighted on deck was promptly attacked by a fierce Alsatian dog. This demonstration of vigilance so impressed him that he retired to his barge with dignity, but without the seat of his pants." Much hilarity dogged Puggy Stephenson after this episode and, relates Chalmers, "the Captain of the frigate is reported to have said that his dog didn't like pugs!"

Undeterred, Stephenson pursued his game of surprise and conquer. "Another time," Chalmers recalls, "while inspecting a Dominion corvette, the Admiral threw his cap on the deck and said: 'That's an unexploded bomb. Take action quick!' Whereupon a young rating broke from the gaping crew and kicked the hat over the side. Showing no surprise, the Admiral commended the lad on his presence of mind; then, pointing to the semi-submerged cap, he said 'That's a survivor—jump in and save him!'" The boy did.

The purpose of Stephenson's sternly disciplinary tactics was to strengthen the trainees' mental and physical defenses against the shock of war and emergency, to imprint on every man of every ship's company an absolute knowledge and understanding of his duties, to train everyone on board to do every job that had to be done. Engineers would find themselves at the guns, cooks hoisting signal flags, and radiomen at the oars of the ship's boat, frantically pulling toward the *Western Isles,* where a sham U-boat crew waited to surrender to a petrified midshipman armed with a rifle and the captain's revolver.

In addition to giving the men of the escort vessels a valuable crash course in their own as well as practically everyone else's duties, the Terror's highly individualistic training program succeeded in welding each crew into a team with confidence in itself and pride in its ship. However much the young officers and men might have cursed the Old Man at Tobermory, he helped many of them to live to tell the tale of his inflicted rigors; and many a ship's captain who had experienced the weight of the Terror's disfavor blessed him later for his iron determination that no ship would join the war at sea until she had reached a standard

that in the commodore's view would give her a reasonable hope of survival.

While the men were improving their skills, however, the convoy system remained flawed. Destroyers desperately needed for the Battle of the Atlantic were held on anti-invasion patrol along the coast. The small number of ships on escort duty still spent far too much time racing off after attackers instead of concentrating their force around the convoy so vulnerable now to Dönitz' wolf-pack strategy. Further weakening the effectiveness of the escort groups was the frequent dispatch, by Western Approaches Command, of units to hunt down U-boats sighted many miles from the convoys that the escorts were supposed to be supporting. Worse, as the by no means unique experience of the *Bluebell* and the *Sturdy* showed, there was scarcely any coordination among the escort ships haphazardly gathered together as they became available for convoy duty, and too little preplanning by headquarters of a course of action to be taken by escorts as a group in case of an attack upon their convoy.

The shock that was induced throughout the Admiralty by the appalling losses of men, ships and matériel was profound. It was obvious that a sound doctrine of protection must be formulated if the convoy system was to work: an unshakable program of team discipline, of coordination and communication among escort ships, of carefully rehearsed procedures to be followed under various conditions of attack. From this realization a new convoy-escort policy slowly emerged.

Starting in the spring of 1941, escort groups would train together and remain together. A number of the destroyers that had been tied up on anti-invasion patrol were released for escort duty. Ashore, radar technicians worked night and day to develop sets that were capable of being fitted onto fleet ships, aircraft and escort vessels. Other specialists concentrated on the development of very-high-frequency radio-telephones, whose signals could be picked up by the Germans only at close range, and high-frequency direction finders to be used for locating wolf packs by their wireless telegraph messages to one another.

The headquarters for Western Approaches Command was moved from Plymouth, which was under continual threat by

German aircraft that were based in France, to Derby House in Liverpool, where Command could be in closer contact with Atlantic shipping and shipmasters. Admiral Sir Percy Noble was appointed new Commander-in-Chief, Western Approaches; and by February 1941, he and his staff were installed in the new operational nerve center.

Sir Percy (page 130) wasted no time in persuading the government to place high priority on the construction of ships, weapons and supporting aircraft. Before the end of his first month as commander-in-chief, he decided to accompany one of the escort groups to find out for himself exactly what was wrong with escort operations and why the convoys were so often left virtually without protection at times when they most needed it. He chose to sail aboard the destroyer of Commander Walter Couchman, senior officer of the escort for that particular convoy. Many years later, one of Couchman's fellow destroyer commanders, by then Captain Donald G. F. Macintyre, was to write an account of that critical voyage:

"Throughout the trip the escorts were subjected to all those interferences by the staff ashore about which we sea-captains had for so long felt bitter. The senior officer was unable to use his own judgment; the ships under his command were sent off in vain chases by orders from ashore, until eventually Couchman's ship with Sir Percy on board was left as the only escort to protect the convoy. No attack developed, but Sir Percy swore he would bring this nonsense to an end. It was a promise he kept and, by doing so, he laid the foundations of victory."

On his return he made it clear to the Admiralty as a whole and his own Western Approaches Command in particular that orders from ashore were to be kept to a minimum: Just give them the information they need, he said in effect; don't tell them what to do.

To ensure that all his officers of whatever rank or branch were indeed capable of exercising their own judgment, Sir Percy prescribed a single specific: "Training, training and then more training."

Activities at Tobermory swung into even higher gear. Almost every ship and every man slated for escort duty, whether a veteran or a landlubber—over a thousand ships' companies by the end of the War—ran Commodore Stephenson's obstacle course. After completing it, each ship and her complement joined the rest of her group at Londonderry or in the River Clyde or Mersey to undergo a period of work-up and training in units that would, whenever possible, be self-contained and permanent. Convoys would be escorted, not by ships thrown together at random and left to the mercy of chance, but by groups of vessels trained to function as teams. Once such a group was formed and trained, it would not be broken up except in cases of extraordinary operational difficulties.

To complement these measures, Sir Percy established a tactical school at Liverpool to train the commanding officers of the escorts in the techniques of convoy protection, U-boat tactics and counterattack procedures. All the commanding officers of each escort group would, again, train as a team, using models and mock-ups to simulate battle conditions. Playing the part of German U-boat commanders, members of the Women's Royal Naval Service—the Wrens—worked the model U-boats while the escort officers, from the vantage points of simulated bridges, went through the drill of coming to grips with the enemy. Afterward a critique was held to determine what had gone wrong, what had gone right, how long it was safe to leave a gap in the protective screen while off hunting attackers, how best to work together and inflict the maximum damage on the marauding submarines.

All that was needed now was more ships, more weapons, more equipment, more sophisticated instruments, more experience, more time.

For the men aboard the convoy escorts, as for the thousands of other men who were fighting the Battle of the Atlantic, the opening weeks of 1941 gave little indication that any significant improvement could be expected in their grim and dangerous lives. While a few additional ships had become available for escort duty, the burden of providing protection for the convoys still fell upon aging destroyers, sloops, corvettes and deep-sea trawlers, which plowed uncomfortably through gale-tossed seas that were almost as tormenting as the enemy.

Among the destroyers, the old British veterans of World War I had been augmented by a few of the sturdier classes that had been built between the wars, and by 50 American "four-stackers" that had been handed over to Great Britain

Raw recruits, some of whom have not even taken off their hats, receive instruction at a merchant marine training base in England from a Royal Navy officer who explains the workings of a 4-inch gun. Gunnery training became essential for Britain's merchant marine as the toll of unarmed merchant ships sunk by German vessels mounted in the first few months of the War. By January 1940, half of Britain's merchant ships were armed with cannon, and could fight back against U-boats.

in exchange for the lease of bases in the West Indies.

The British destroyers were stout, speedy ships, but they had been originally designed for use in the North Sea, and their fuel capacity was limited. Until an extra fuel tank could be fitted in the space provided by the removal of one boiler—a dockyard job, taking each ship out of action for weeks when she was most needed—they were capable of shepherding a convoy no more than a few hundred miles out to sea before having to turn back with a homeward-bound convoy. Their timeworn engines required devoted and continuous attention; their hulls trembled convulsively in heavy seas, and rivets burst from their plates, permitting icy water to spurt into the crew's quarters, soaking everything and making life all but unbearable. It was from the tiny bridges of these ships, unprotected except for canvas sheets that were sometimes swept away early in each trip, that the escort commanders endeavored to guide their flocks through the treacherous sea.

The 50 American destroyers were, if anything, even more uncomfortable than their British counterparts. They filled a vital need, bridging the gap between what was previously available and what was essential, and without them Britain might well have lost the Battle of the Atlantic in its most critical phase. But there were times when the British crews aboard felt that perhaps that alternative might not be so terrible, at least for themselves.

The American four-stackers had a roll that put one startled observer in mind of a windshield wiper operating at top speed. Their aging machinery was in frequent need of repair; their weapons were obsolete. With a turning circle as broad as that of a battleship, the destroyers inevitably caught the huge North Atlantic seas abeam at some point as they turned to head for port. The results were unpleasant at best, and sometimes disastrous. The low, glassed-in bridges caught every high sea, which often shattered the windows. During such moments the ship had to be guided by men who were virtually waist-deep in water and lashed to the nearest stanchion.

When the Royal Navy officers and crew crossed the Atlantic to take over the ships, they found to their intense surprise and gratitude that the United States Navy, in a gesture of generosity toward their hard-pressed colleagues, had fitted out the ships with luxuries almost unheard-of in the British

Navy. Cabins and crew's quarters were stocked with cigarettes, matches, blankets, sheets and cushions; the storerooms were full of steaks and bacon; washrooms were equipped with toothpaste, soap and towels. It was a moment for much thankfulness.

But at sea during a particularly violent winter gale, an aggrieved watchkeeping officer was heard to say: "Look! I know we've smoked all their Camels, but if we offered them a thousand Players, do you think they'd take this bloody sieve back?"

Britain's own sloops could also be extremely uncomfortable. Some were of the prewar type; others were of the newer Black Swan class that first came to sea, in limited numbers, just after the beginning of the War. The prewar class sloops had a maximum speed of 16 knots—not enough to overtake a surfaced submarine. But they had been designed for long voyages and were in no danger of running out of fuel if their convoy time was extended by rerouting or bad weather. Unfortunately, having originally been fitted out to serve as gunboats in the tropics, or for minesweeping work with the Mediterranean and Far Eastern fleets, they proved excessively cold for crews on duty off the coast of Iceland or Newfoundland.

The later Black Swan sloops offered scarcely better protection against wintry blasts, but were otherwise superbly suited for convoy duty. Capable of a speed of 19 knots and carrying six 4-inch antiaircraft guns, they were much in demand for convoys going to Gibraltar when the Luftwaffe joined the battle across the Bay of Biscay from bases in western France.

The corvettes, however, bore the main escort burden. And the greater part of this burden fell on the Flower class—vessels improbably named after the gentle and delicate flowers of the British garden. The wise Lords of the Admiralty would not permit a corvette to be christened the H.M.S. Pansy, but the Daffodil, the Hyacinth, the Periwinkle and the Meadowsweet were all to win battle honors in the most bitter theater of the ocean war, as were their sister ships with even more striking names, such as the Campanula and the Coreopsis.

Broad-beamed and solid, corvettes stood up to the North Atlantic battering far better than destroyers did, although their single reciprocating "push-and-pull" engines could manage a top speed of only 15 knots. This hampered the corvettes in their pursuit of surfaced U-boats, which were able to travel at a top speed of 17 to 18 knots, but their maneuverability made them perfect for maintaining asdic contact with submerged submarines. Even more important than their toughness and handiness was the fact that they were easy to build and could be produced quickly. It was on the combination of large numbers of corvettes sliding down the launching ways and of even larger numbers of sailors going through the Tobermory mill that the hopes of the future depended.

But the corvettes were even more uncomfortable than the sloops and American destroyers. As Nicholas Monsarrat later commented somewhat sourly, "a corvette would roll on wet grass." Anyone who had the slightest tendency toward seasickness, like Commander Sherwood's young officers on the Bluebell, would suffer for the first few days of every voyage, adding immeasurably to the discomfort of the rest of the crew. Even on a relatively calm sea, there was no possibility of relaxation. The physical strain probably shortened the lives of everyone who served on a corvette. Wherever a man stood, sat, lay, worked or moved, he had to hang on to something or someone. Even then some piece of loosened gear was likely to hurl into him, knocking the wind out of him, cracking his ribs, bruising his shins, mashing his fingers.

In bad weather and during U-boat alerts—both of which were frequent in the first quarter of 1941—there was no rest for the men of the corvettes. And the three or four hours they snatched for sleep were invariably spent clinging to the bunks, wedged in by sodden blankets. "When we got back home," Sherwood remembers, "all we wanted to do was to lay our heads down and catch up on sleep."

Practically anything that could float was used to swell the ranks of the escorts. Trawlers—as many as could be spared from their primary task of supplying fish to Britain—were commandeered by the Admiralty and fitted out with asdic, a gun or two, and a brace of depth-charge racks. They were slow, their armament was small, and their score against the U-boats was negligible. Still they performed valiant service in rescuing the crews of sinking ships while the better-equipped and faster escort vessels took on the Germans.

Somehow, all of these oddly assorted ships managed to work together with some success in the days before relief arrived in the shape of additional fast escorts, then being built in the shipyards.

After the bad weather of January and February, 1941, which had called for sharply curtailed operations, March brought calmer seas, and the U-boats swung back into action. British losses accelerated at a disastrous rate. About half a million tons of shipping were lost to surface, air and underwater raiders. Submarines alone accounted for 41 ships, many of them stragglers.

But in the same month a series of significant events occurred to encourage the belief that some of the lessons learned by the Admiralty were beginning to take effect.

Convoy OB-293, outward-bound from Liverpool to Halifax, reached an area some hundreds of miles to the south of Iceland in the first week of March. The chattering of German radios—picked up by Britain's direction-finding stations on shore—had made it possible for the Admiralty to warn the convoy's escorts that U-boats were gathering in the vicinity. At dusk on March 6, submarines led by Günther Prien in the U-47 attacked OB-293 and kept up the assault for 24 hours. Two merchantmen were sunk and two more damaged. But the convoy escorts, led by the old World War I destroyer Wolverine, under Commander James Rowland, turned on the attackers with deadly ferocity, and this time a price was exacted.

First, one of the older U-boats was hit by depth charges and was so shaken that her commander, Hans Eckermann, had no choice but to drop out of the battle—which he managed to do in the general confusion—and limp slowly back to Lorient.

Then the U-70, under Lieut. Commander Joachim Matz, was brought to the surface after a grueling chase by the corvettes Camellia and Arbutus. So badly damaged was his submarine that he ordered the crew to abandon ship after demolition charges in the hull had been set off. The new-found efficiency of the convoy's escort was such that even the U-99, under the redoubtable Otto Kretschmer, was driven off with only half its torpedoes fired.

But Prien in the U-47 remained, doggedly shadowing the convoy, determined not to let the quarry elude him while he still possessed the means of inflicting damage. On the 8th of March, even though the seas were heavy and the skies were overcast, he prepared to make his move. During the day, he watched the convoy, fervently hoping that it would not disperse; and then, surfacing in thick weather and fading light, which hid his small craft from the lookouts, he closed in. Just before dusk, under cover of a helpful rain squall, Prien penetrated the escort screen. Then his luck suddenly deserted him. The squall ended abruptly, momentarily whipping away the leaden clouds, and under the last rays of a dying sun the destroyer Wolverine and the U-47 stood naked in each other's view.

There was a blinding moment of mutual consternation and astonishment. Prien, his advantage so unexpectedly reversed, collected himself and swung the U-47 away in an effort to escape on the surface. The Wolverine surged after her as Commander Rowland called for all the power the old engines could give him. Undoubtedly they could give him enough to overtake the U-boat if Prien maintained a straight course; but the U-47 had much greater maneuverability than the destroyer and had every chance of dodging away—especially with night coming on to further reduce the already uncertain visibility.

But then, to Rowland's surprise, Prien took the U-47 down in a crash dive, and she was immediately picked up by the Wolverine's asdic. The first pattern of depth charges, set shallow, could hardly miss; and as their crash and rumble died away, the hydrophone operators heard from below the persistent rattle of propeller shafts out of alignment. The U-47 was in dire trouble, and it was now just a question of waiting.

When darkness fell, Prien surfaced again. The Wolverine, a mile away and still tracking the U-47's propeller rattle, increased speed in Prien's direction. Again the crash dive; again the pattern of depth charges at shallow setting—this time followed by a thunderous explosion and a dazzling flare of light bursting up from below. In a little while, bits and pieces of debris churned to the surface: indisputable evidence of a destroyed U-boat. For the first time in the Battle of the Atlantic, a convoy escort had trumped an ace. Günther Prien was gone.

The U-47 was not the last British trophy of that month. On the afternoon of March 16, Convoy HX-112, with more than

50 heavily loaded merchantmen heading for the Western Approaches, was well into the danger area, and aware of it. The previous night it had lost a 10,000-ton tanker in an appalling explosion that had shot flames hundreds of feet into the air and then covered the sullen waters with a carpet of fire. The escort leader, Commander Donald Macintyre, had no reason to doubt that during the coming night the ships of his convoy would almost certainly be subjected to fierce attack.

His command, a newly formed escort group, consisted of his own ship, the *Walker*, four more destroyers—the *Vanoc*, the *Volunteer*, the *Sardonyx* and the *Scimitar*—plus the corvettes *Bluebell* and *Hydrangea*. Although Macintyre did not doubt the eagerness and determination of the men who were under his command, he was worried about their relative lack of battle experience. There was a considerable amount of tension aboard the command ship as evening approached, and it was with some relief that Macintyre received the signal from the *Scimitar*: "Submarine in sight six miles ahead."

Off sped the *Walker*, the *Vanoc* and the *Scimitar*, hoping to get within range before being spotted by the U-boat's lookout. No one was surprised, however, when the enemy crash-dived while the escort vessels were still some three miles away. What was surprising, though, and frustrating, was that no sign of an asdic contact was reported by any of the operators. After an hour's tedious and exasperating hunt, the chagrined Macintyre ordered the *Walker* to return to the convoy to fill at least one of the gaps left in the protective screen.

By 10 p.m. the *Walker* had rejoined the convoy, and Macintyre, hoping that the *Vanoc* and the *Scimitar* were holding the enemy down, ordered the convoy to make a radical change of course in the hope of losing the U-boat altogether. At 10:06 p.m. an explosion shattered his hopes as one of the ships in the convoy was hit. Four additional explosions followed within the next hour as torpedoes found their targets.

"I was near to despair," Macintyre remembered, "and I racked my brains to find some way to stop the holocaust. While the convoy stayed in impeccable formation, we escorts raced about in the exasperating business of searching in vain for the almost invisible enemy. Our one hope was to sight a U-boat's tell-tale white wake, give chase to force her to dive, and so give the asdics a chance to bring our depth-charges into action. Everything had to be subordinated to that end and so, with binoculars firmly wedged on a steady bearing, I put *Walker* into a gently curving course, thereby putting every point of the compass under a penetrating probe." The maneuver worked. "As her bows swung, a thin line of white water came into the lens of my glasses, a thin line which could only be the wake of a ship. There were none of ours in that direction; it had to be a U-boat!"

The *Walker* surged up to full power and gave chase. The U-boat crash-dived, and moments later the depth charges, so hard upon the target that it seemed they could not miss, sent their plumes of water high into the air. But search as the escorts would, they found no concrete evidence to prove a "kill." Disappointed but determined, Macintyre stayed in the area, asdic still in operation, probing the depths for proof of success or failure.

Macintyre found evidence of failure half an hour later in the form of a firm contact much nearer the convoy—for the U-boat, with commendable determination, had crept back to resume her assault. The *Vanoc* now teamed up with the *Walker* to scour the area systematically and to bombard it

British Captain Donald G. F. Macintyre—a pilot as well as a destroyer commander—developed sub-killing tactics that were widely adopted in World War II. During a single night in March 1941, he captured Germany's greatest submarine ace, Otto Kretschmer, and forced to the surface another submarine, commanded by ace Joachim Schepke. Schepke's boat was rammed by a British ship, and he died in the collision.

with depth charges, none of which had any visible effect although they must surely have shaken the submarine severely. Eventually the waters were in such turmoil that asdic was no longer effective, and Macintyre ordered a temporary halt. With the *Vanoc* circling around as guard, the *Walker* stopped and picked up the survivors of one of the ships that had been torpedoed.

Course had just been set for a return to the search area when the *Vanoc* suddenly raced off at full speed, the signal lights on her bridge flashing an almost unreadable message as she plowed ahead. Within moments it became obvious to Macintyre that she had spotted the U-boat, now limping along on the surface. It was an incredible feat, for no human eye could see that far—with or without binoculars—on a North Atlantic winter's night. Macintyre was only later to learn how the *Vanoc* had accomplished it.

The next few moments were dramatic: as the *Vanoc* surged up to full power, lookouts could see the U-boat trying to turn away from her but clearly in trouble. The submarine made no attempt to dive; crew members were on deck running toward the 4-inch gun, presumably intending to turn it on the destroyer. But there was no time to bring it into action. As the *Vanoc* continued to move forward, the U-boat disappeared from sight under the overhang of the destroyer's bows; there was a shout, and a crashing noise, and as the men on the *Vanoc*'s deck ran to the side and looked down, they saw the U-boat turn over and sink away into the depths.

One of the *Vanoc*'s crew had a fleeting glimpse of the side of the conning tower as the U-boat submerged for the last time. On it was painted "U-100"—the submarine commanded by ace Joachim Schepke. Crushed to death by the *Vanoc*'s bow, Schepke had gone to join Prien.

While the *Vanoc* picked up the few survivors, the *Walker* circled protectively. Then, from the *Walker*'s asdic operator, came the cry of "Contact! Contact!" Skepticism combined with apprehension ruled on the bridge, the first because of the likelihood of mistaking the wreckage and turbulent waters from the recent killing for a genuine contact; and the second because the supply of depth charges on the deck had been depleted during the hunt for the *U-100* and was only now being replaced from the magazine—a cumbersome and time-consuming process. But the asdic operator was positive that another U-boat had arrived on the scene, so the *Walker* turned and attacked again with the seven depth charges that the crew had been able to prepare on such short notice. Almost immediately there was a signal from the *Vanoc*—"U-boat surfaced astern of me"—and her searchlight shot out to reveal the wallowing shape of a submarine in trouble.

Gunfire crackled from the *Walker* and the *Vanoc*. A signal lamp from the U-boat's conning tower flashed a message that was not quite English but was nevertheless unmistakable. "We are sunking," it said.

One after another German seaman leaped into the icy water. As they started swimming, their abandoned boat lifted her stern and slid under. The *Walker*'s crew lowered the scrambling nets, and the men of the U-boat, half-frozen and close to exhaustion, clambered clumsily aboard.

The last man up the nets wore a resplendent captain's cap, and from his neck dangled a pair of exceptionally fine Zeiss binoculars worn only by an exclusive few. He was Lieut. Commander Otto Kretschmer, the Reich's top-scoring U-boat ace—with 266,629 tons of shipping to his credit.

Within a few days, in the month of March, British escort ships had bagged Germany's three top U-boat aces.

March, then, despite the frightening toll of Allied merchant shipping losses, was not a total disaster for the hard-pressed Britons. The convoy-escort system was truly beginning to prove itself.

Perhaps even more significant than the dispatch of the three submarines was the manner in which the *U-100* was sighted by the destroyer *Vanoc*. For the first time, a surfaced U-boat had been "seen" by means other than the human eye. Rudimentary as yet, and not fully understood by its operators, a newly installed radar set on the *Vanoc* had detected the *U-100* at a distance well beyond the vision of even the youngest and keenest lookouts. This could mean, and would mean, that surfaced U-boats, traveling singly or in packs, in the daytime or at night, could no longer count on the advantage of surprise, nor would they be able to so easily elude pursuit.

Although it would not be completely evident for many months to come, a turning point had been reached in the Battle of the Atlantic.

JOURNEYS INTO DANGER

Cargo-laden Victory ships in a Europe-bound convoy plow through stormy seas after a gale in the North Atlantic, a favorite stalking ground for U-boats.

RUNNING THE U-BOAT GAUNTLET

A crewman on an Allied escort destroyer maintains vigilance even while off duty, aware that a convoy was always most vulnerable in fair weather.

Even in perfect weather, herding a compact formation of 30 to 40 ships across the Atlantic Ocean without a collision or some other major mishap would have been a feat. But in winter the undertaking demanded a superhuman effort. The main convoy route cut through a region of the North Atlantic where some of the world's foulest weather prevails between November and April. Ships that were jacketed with ice or blinded by snow struggled to keep their places in the formation; in thick fog, vessels were shielded from U-boats but risked ramming one another or their own circling escorts. Seas up to 60 feet high could break the backs of ships and smash lifeboats to splinters, while winds of hurricane strength tested the wills of haggard skippers. Men who were blown or washed overboard often froze to death in a matter of seconds.

To keep one ship on course under such circumstances was trying; to synchronize the passage of scores of ships for up to two weeks in the face of U-boats and dismal weather required the utmost skill and tenacity.

Even in the most difficult circumstances, peak alertness had to be maintained. At night, crews kept bone-aching vigils, searching the white wave caps for a conning tower. By day, they hunted periscopes with binoculars in tedious but methodical patterns, each man searching a small quadrant of sea again and again.

Always the strain and the exhaustion were mingled with fear. Round-the-clock vigilance was no guarantee that a torpedo would not strike at any moment. Emboldened by success, U-boats might even surface in the middle of a convoy to slaughter ships all around.

In October 1940, a year after the War began, Convoy SC-7 lost 16 ships out of 35 in one attack. As the War progressed, shipping losses mounted. In May of 1942, U-boats sank 120 Allied ships, and in June they accounted for another 119. And before the Battle of the Atlantic would end, Great Britain would lose more than 32,000 of its merchant seamen, almost one fourth of the total number who served in its forces during all of World War II.

A convoy off the English coast tows barrage balloons to ward off German aircraft. The steel cables could slice wings and shatter props.

Alert to the presence of another ship looming dangerously close in heavy fog, the deck officer of a convoy escort keeps a sharp lookout beside his signal lamp for other ships. Collisions in which loaded ships went quickly to the ocean bottom were a major hazard for convoys that were caught in Atlantic fog banks.

High seas and gale winds batter the cruiser H.M.S. Bellona on escort duty near Norway. Convoys welcomed storms that grounded enemy planes.

In below-zero weather on a convoy run in the North Atlantic, crew members bundle up against the searing cold on their ice-encrusted cargo vessel.

An Allied ship in the middle of a convoy suffers a torpedo hit during an attack by Luftwaffe planes. The torpedo track is the white line leading to the ship's bow

at right center; another track passes the bow harmlessly. The photograph was taken from a German plane, whose wing strut appears in the foreground.

Torpedoed amidships, a tanker becomes an inferno of fuel oil. Tankers carried the convoy's most valuable cargo and received the best protection.

A tanker crew plays a hose on a blaze. Their quick action saved this ship, which was then towed to an American port for repairs.

Safely home from submarine-infested waters, a convoy moves toward the Thames estuary as sea gulls form a welcoming escort. When convoys neared the British

Isles, land-based aircraft took over protective duties; warships then peeled off and sped ahead into port, where their exhausted crews got a well-earned rest.

5

When, within the short space of 10 days in March 1941, three of Germany's top U-boat aces, Günther Prien, Joachim Schepke and Otto Kretschmer, were eliminated from the War, a deep sense of satisfaction flowed through the embattled Royal Navy. What few of the rank and file realized at the time was that a new device had helped knock out Schepke's *U-100*. That device was of course radar, and it was only the first of several advances in antisubmarine warfare that began to give the British reason to think that the advantage was at last shifting to their side in the Battle of the Atlantic.

Until the appearance of radar, U-boats had been able to rise to the surface at night and attack Allied shipping with impunity. Once on the surface, they could not be located by asdic but only by the human eye. And in the concealing darkness, they were frequently able to steal up on convoys without being noticed, fire their torpedoes and guns, and then sneak away.

But once radar was installed on the escort vessels that accompanied the convoys, the U-boats could no longer count on such easy pickings—or on so easy an escape. Radar could see in the dark, and in foul weather as well. Asdic and radar working in tandem could track submarines both above and below the surface, enabling the escort ships to move in on them.

Ironically, the principle on which radar was based had first been discovered by a German scientist, Heinrich Hertz. In 1886, Hertz detected the existence of radio waves; later he determined that they are reflected by solid objects, and this discovery led many years later to the development of transmitting sets that could bounce radio waves off solid objects and then pick up the returning impulses. The term *radar* evolved from the words "Radio Detection and Ranging": by the use of radar an object could not only be detected, but also its range could be determined by measuring the time that it took for the reflected waves to come back to the sending set. And if the object under investigation happened to be moving, its speed and direction of movement could also be determined.

In the years before World War II, scientists in Germany, Britain, France and the United States had been working on radar. The British effort dated from the winter of 1934-1935, when the Air Ministry set up a committee to study ways of

THE TRIUMPH OF TECHNOLOGY

improving the country's air defense. An experimental radar system was installed at Orfordness, on the east coast of England, in the spring of 1935, and in 1936 construction was begun on a network of five air warning radar stations around the Thames estuary. By 1940 a line of radar stations had been strung along the southern and eastern coasts of the island kingdom. These stations played a key role in the great air clashes of the summer and fall of 1940 that came to be known as the Battle of Britain. By providing the Royal Air Force with early warnings of approaching Luftwaffe squadrons and by revealing the number and direction of the bombers, they made it possible for RAF fighters to respond quickly and effectively.

Shipboard radar was longer in coming about. The first sets did not begin reaching units of the Royal Navy until early 1941. Their antennae were crude, ungainly contraptions that many a ship's captain accepted with almost as much disdain as gratitude. On these early sets only one target could be read at a time. Contact showed up as a "pip" on a green line that ran across the screen of an oscilloscope. The bearing of the target could be read from the direction of the antenna—which in the first sets did not rotate—and the range could be determined from the position of the pip on the oscilloscope. At least that was the theory. In practice, early radar was more useful in helping a skipper maintain his assigned station in a convoy screen during periods of poor visibility (it warned him that he was steaming too close to or too far from the ships he was escorting) than in pinpointing U-boats.

A less complicated electronic detection device was also in use among Britain's antisubmarine forces. This was the ship-borne high-frequency direction finder—British sailors called it "Huff-Duff" from its initials. Except for radar, no single invention would prove more telling in the struggle against the U-boats.

Prewar navigators had employed radio direction finders to take bearings on shore stations, using low and medium frequencies only. Huff-Duff, on the other hand, could tune in on the high-frequency coded transmissions—and therefore also on the coded messages—that Admiral Dönitz' U-boats used to communicate with headquarters. To zero in on these signals, shore-based direction-finding stations were established on both sides of the Atlantic and in Iceland and Greenland. When two or more of these widely separated stations picked up a radio message that was sent by a U-boat at sea, the cross-bearings that resulted revealed the approximate position of the submarine.

This information was relayed to a central point, the Submarine Tracking Room set up by the Admiralty in London. There, special teams analyzed and plotted the positions and movements of the U-boats. As the tracking teams became adept, they were able to compile a remarkably accurate picture of U-boat dispositions throughout the North Atlantic. Each day they sent coded bulletins to the convoy escorts, telling them where the wolf packs were lying in wait. Thus forewarned, the convoys often were able to change course in time to avoid attack.

Huff-Duff took advantage of an inherent weakness in German submarine tactics. Dönitz' system of central control made regular radio communication between the U-boats and their headquarters necessary. Had the subs maintained radio silence, they would not have been able to send messages to home base and home base would not have known when to order the U-boats to come together and close in for a wolf-pack attack.

There was another weakness in Dönitz' system as well: German submariners chattered back and forth with headquarters on the radio, enabling the Admiralty to determine the positions of their U-boats. Even the briefest message could give away a submarine's location. British operators were able sometimes to get a fix on nothing more substantial than a coded message containing figures. Even when the Germans became aware that the British possessed some new weapon, efforts to hold down the volume of radio traffic had little effect, partly because the submariners never realized that the convoy escort vessels themselves had been fitted with Huff-Duff, and partly because the wolf-pack system relied on radio transmissions to concentrate the pack on the target.

By mid-1941 the British were making use of the content of German radio transmissions as well as the signals themselves. The submarine U-110 had been captured by British escort vessels on convoy duty off Greenland in May, and had yielded intact a German electronic coding machine. Cryptanalysts of the super-secret Ultra group used the captured machine to break the German naval code. Henceforth, although the Germans were not aware of it, many of their most sensitive radio messages were being read in the Admiralty.

When the ship-borne version of Huff-Duff appeared, it enabled two ships of an escort to get their own fix on a submarine with much greater accuracy than shore stations hundreds of miles away could provide, and to close in together for a depth-charge attack.

As the means by which ships could detect submarines were improved, so were methods of communication between ships sailing in the same convoy. When darkness or fog made visual signaling impractical, the only alternative available had been coded radio messages that required more time and skilled personnel to transmit and receive than could be afforded in battle conditions. A solution was found in the very-high-frequency radio-telephone, which made it possible for a radioman, watch officer or ship's captain to talk directly to nearby ships during an attack.

Eventually, radio-telephone also could be used between ships and aircraft, thus improving the teamwork between air and surface escorts.

Some of the advances that were made in antisubmarine warfare came not from new inventions, but simply by improving old detection devices and visual aids. To increase visibility during nighttime attacks, escort ships in the early part of the War fired star shells over the area in which they believed a surfaced submarine was lurking. But the shells did not provide much light and the flash of the gun that was used to fire them momentarily blinded the ship's lookouts and impaired their night vision, making it extremely difficult for them to see in the dark thereafter until their eyes had adjusted again to the darkness.

An early answer to this challenge was the "snowflake," a rocket that could be fired into the air with minimal flash. The explosion it made left a strong white light lingering in the sky for several minutes. All of the ships in the convoy received a supply of snowflakes with orders to fire them in

unison upon a prearranged signal during a U-boat attack.

The combined firing could light up the sea for miles around; if there were U-boats lurking in the area, they were often starkly revealed. Snowflakes were two-edged weapons, however, because they also made clearer targets of the ships that fired them. Still, it was kill or be killed, and if snowflakes gave the escorts the chance to fire the first shots or release their depth charges on target, they were worth the risk.

One elementary change that greatly enhanced the survival rate of ships in convoys came not from any breakthrough or improvement in military hardware, but from a careful analysis of sinkings. Operational Research, a little-noted backroom unit of the Admiralty, concluded that the number of vessels lost in any convoy depended upon the number of attacking submarines and the size of the escort, and was not in any way related to the number of ships there were in the convoy.

For example, if a wolf pack attacked a convoy of 20 ships and sank 10, it did not follow that the same wolf pack attacking a convoy of 70 ships would sink 35. It would, in fact, probably sink no more than 10; a much greater proportion of a large convoy would get through safely.

As a result of this study, the British sharply increased the size of a typical convoy from about 30 ships to 50, 60 and sometimes even more. This also meant that more escort vessels could be allotted to each convoy and that there would be fewer convoys at sea at any one time for the submarines to attack.

Larger convoys did mean a larger area for the escorts to defend—a seeming disadvantage. But basic geometry demonstrated that two small convoys had in fact more exposed perimeter to be protected than did one convoy twice the size. As luck would have it, this basic discovery came at a time when the number of escort vessels available for convoy duty was rising.

The twin problems of providing enough escort vessels for the convoys and of extending adequate protection all the way across the Atlantic were greatly eased by the Canadian contribution to the Allied effort. When the War began, the Royal Canadian Navy was little more than a token force: six destroyers, five minesweepers and some 3,000 officers and men. Yet by 1941, Canada had taken full responsibility for

guarding the convoys on the western leg of the Atlantic run. It could do so because of an ambitious ship-building and training program launched by Prime Minister Mackenzie King; before the War was over, Canada would send almost 400 ships and 90,000 Canadians to sea.

The potency of air power as a weapon against submarines had been proved in World War I, but like so many lessons of that war it had to be learned all over again in the Second World War. When the British organized a convoy system in 1917, they reduced their shipping losses by 80 per cent. And when aircraft—even the primitive planes of that era—were added to the convoy escorts to spot and attack lurking U-boats, the losses became almost negligible. Out of all the ships that were protected by air cover, only five were sunk by the Kaiser's U-boats.

In World War II, it soon became evident to the Allies that the approach of one of their planes, even one that carried no effective weapons, had an electrifying effect on a surfaced U-boat. The submarine usually dived as fast as she could for the safety of deep water. And the dive cost her opportunities. The submerged U-boat found it much harder to detect approaching ships. And if she were tracking a convoy, she was much more likely to lose contact underwater, because her speed was greatly reduced. If the plane's sighting report brought escort ships to the scene quickly enough, they could use their asdic to seek out the submarine and attack her.

In the years between wars, the British had done little to prepare their air arm for a war against submarines. Aside from the fact that the U-boat menace was not considered a major threat by the military planners, there were relatively few pilots available who had been trained for sub spotting in any case. Before the end of the First World War, the Royal Naval Air Service had been absorbed into the RAF, and in the intervening years few pilots had been trained in naval aviation of any kind.

With the establishment of the Fleet Air Arm in 1937, the Royal Navy regained control of its own air wing, but only so far as carrier planes were concerned. The RAF's land-based Coastal Command was still responsible for all other maritime aircraft, and the Navy remained the orphan of British aviation. The planes assigned to the Navy generally were

Clothed against flashback, a British sailor in a foul-weather coat helps ready a depth charge for firing aboard the corvette Rhododendron. Ship's officers (background) search the water for evidence of the success of previous firings. The explosive-filled cans were rolled off the stern and fired off the sides. The resulting diamond-shaped patterns generally consisted of 14 charges, enough to encompass a submarine.

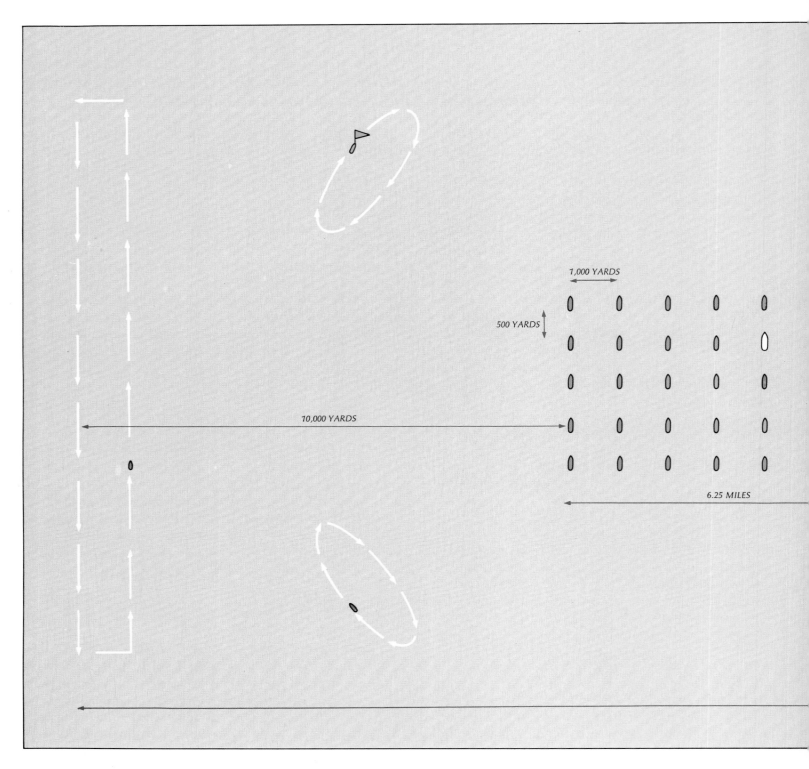

1,000 YARDS

500 YARDS

10,000 YARDS

6.25 MILES

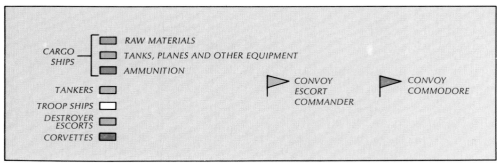

CARGO SHIPS — RAW MATERIALS

TANKS, PLANES AND OTHER EQUIPMENT

AMMUNITION

TANKERS

TROOP SHIPS

DESTROYER ESCORTS

CORVETTES

CONVOY ESCORT COMMANDER

CONVOY COMMODORE

DIAGRAM FOR A WINNING COMBINATION

When the War was over, Admiral Karl Dönitz wrote: "The German submarine campaign was wrecked by the introduction of the convoy system." Diagramed above is a typical 1942 convoy, whose formation made it difficult for U-boats to score a kill, even at night when they could operate on the surface.

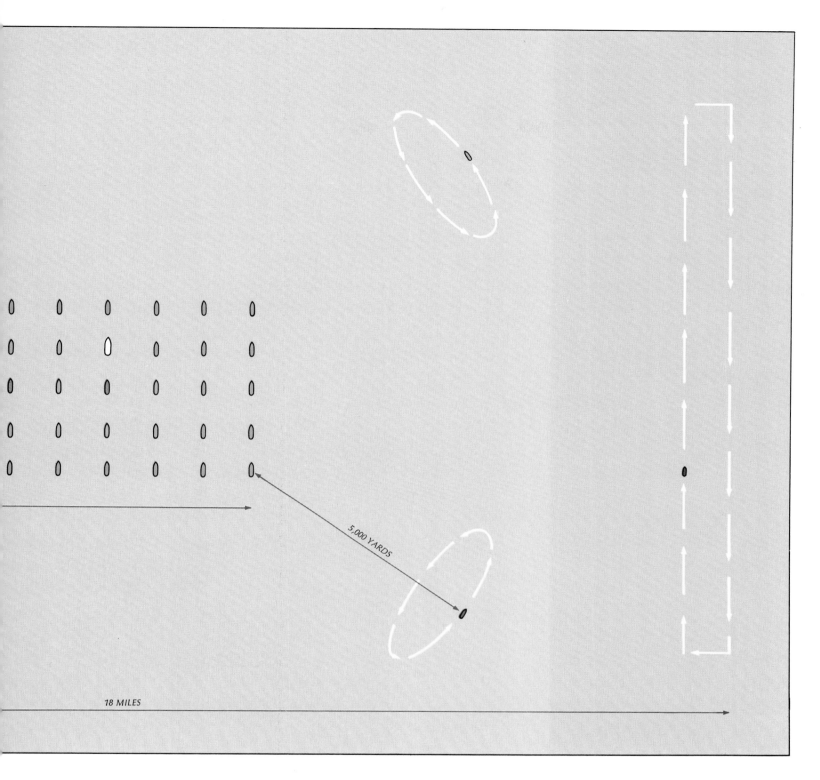

5,000 YARDS

18 MILES

Because the merchant ships presented the biggest target from bow to stern, the convoy's vessels were deployed only five deep, thereby minimizing the number exposed to flank attack. Oil tankers, troop transports, ammunition ships and vessels loaded with tanks, guns and other vital war matériel were placed inside the formation. (Ammunition ships were never positioned next to one another—or to oil tankers—for fear a torpedo hit might set off a chain reaction of explosions or fires.) Around the convoy's core were cargo ships carrying expendable raw materials (cotton, wheat, ore). Ships were spread over an area 18 miles wide and spaced carefully to provide maximum safety while maintaining close contact with one another.

In this typical formation the convoy is accompanied by two destroyer escorts and four corvettes. The destroyers patrol in elliptical patterns to prevent attacks from the front, while two corvettes guard the rear. The other corvettes patrol its flanks.

The convoy commodore, who was responsible for the merchant vessels and saw to it that they maintained their positions, rode front and center. The escort commander also rode up front, but on the convoy's portside. Under U-boat attack, the escort commander took charge of the entire convoy, issuing orders to the convoy commodore, even when outranked.

RAF castoffs, or aircraft originally designed for land use that had to be modified drastically for carrier duty and were so vulnerable and tricky to fly that their pilots referred to them as "flying coffins."

When the War began, RAF Coastal Command was in sole charge of protecting shipping and patrolling the waters off the British Isles from the air. But Coastal Command also was neglected. At the start of the War, it had only 170 multi-engine seaplanes and conventional land-based planes available for antisubmarine duty, most of them obsolete, with limited range and combat effectiveness.

Moreover, Coastal Command's plight could not improve in those early days. First priority in the building of new aircraft and the training of men to fly them went to RAF Fighter Command, which used its resources heroically in the air battles over Britain in 1940. After that, the inauguration of the strategic bombing campaign against the German homeland led to a massive build-up of RAF Bomber Command. A few naval voices argued that the resources devoted to the bombing of German cities could be used more profitably in the battle against submarines. The voices went unheeded, and after more than a year of war, Coastal Command possessed barely 50 more planes than it had when the fighting started.

In addition to the shortage of planes and trained men, Coastal Command suffered severely from poorly conceived

tactics in the same way that the Navy did. Instead of being deployed just above or reasonably close to the convoys —and thus discouraging the U-boats by their presence— the airplanes were more frequently dispatched independently on wide sweeps of the empty ocean. It was the old "search and patrol" doctrine all over again, and the results of such missions were just as unrewarding from the air as they had been on the sea.

When a plane did happen across a surfaced submarine, the pilot had no effective weapons with which to attack her. At the outbreak of war, planes sent out on antisubmarine duty were supplied with small bombs, but they were not equipped with bombsights. The bombs had to be dropped from very low altitudes, and pilots had to rely on their eyes alone to aim them.

The hazards of this system were dramatically illustrated on the 14th of September, 1939, when two dive bombers from the British carrier *Ark Royal* spotted a German U-boat that was cruising on the surface. The submarine, under the direction of Lieut. Commander Fritz-Julius Lemp, was homeward-bound after having been responsible for the sinking of the British passenger liner *Athenia*. The pilots dived as low as they dared, let go their bombs and began to climb away—only to discover that their bombs had skipped over the surface of the ocean and bounced up into the air underneath the planes. The fuses had been activated by the impact of the bounce, and the bombs exploded, spraying

the planes with shrapnel and forcing the pilots to ditch in the Atlantic. Lieut. Commander Lemp picked up the two men and took them back to Germany aboard his submarine.

The incident of the bouncing bombs was repeated more than once until the British perfected an effective airborne depth charge. It was an adaptation of the Navy's depth charge, fitted with fins and a rounded nose to give it more stable flight, and set not to explode until it reached a certain depth underwater.

But depth charges dropped from the air had to explode close to a U-boat if they were to inflict any serious damage on her steel hull. This was not easy when the target was moving and could suddenly disappear beneath the surface in a crash dive. Experience born of missed opportunities gradually taught the airmen that their only real chance for a kill was to concentrate their firepower by dropping a number of depth charges all at once while the submarine was close beneath the surface—25 feet was about the limit of effectiveness.

As 1941 got under way, the planners were beginning to recognize the importance of air power in the antisubmarine campaign. Coastal Command was given more and better aircraft; included were some 30 American-built Catalina flying boats, which could cruise for 17 to 25 hours at a time. With new equipment and growing experience, the pilots became increasingly battle-wise. One simple trick involved painting the undersides of planes white instead of black,

which made them more difficult to see against the sky.

In the spring, operational control of Coastal Command was turned over to the Admiralty. This assured the Navy of top-priority air support, while leaving the officers and men of Coastal Command in the RAF, where they traditionally belonged. With summer, air coverage in the Atlantic was improved. A squadron of Lockheed Hudsons, another squadron of old seaplanes and a third of long-range fighters began flying air cover out of Iceland, thus reducing by 400 miles the part of the mid-ocean convoy routes that was beyond the reach of protective aircraft.

The effectiveness of airplanes as antisubmarine weapons was severely limited in the early part of the War by their inability to spot their targets at night. Early attempts to equip Coastal Command planes with radar in 1940 had failed. But scientists had persevered and by 1941 many planes were being fitted with cumbersome sets that required mounting large antennae on either side of a plane's rear fuselage, two smaller forward-looking antennae underneath the wings and reflectors built on posts on top of the fuselage to receive the return signals. Inside the plane a member of the crew—usually the navigator or radio operator—had the additional duty of monitoring the radar screen. On one type of plane, the Whitley, used by Coastal Command, the new equipment was installed in such a way that to use it the operator had to sit on the seat of the plane's toilet, midway along the cold and dank tunnel of the cabin. It was not popular duty.

Early airborne radar—known as ASV, for air to surface vessel—had another limitation: it lost contact when the target came too close. At a range of about one mile, the blip that indicated the position of the submarine disappeared from the screen. On a dark night, a U-boat could escape. But the gap was eventually bridged by adding a powerful searchlight to each plane. The technical problems of developing such a light were overcome by the ingenuity of an RAF officer named Humphrey de Verde Leigh. Squadron Leader Leigh had been a pilot in World War I but had been relegated to a desk job at Coastal Command headquarters because of his age. Leigh heard about the radar-gap dilemma almost by accident and, being a determined fellow, set about to invent a light that could be mounted under an aircraft. He came up with one that was powered by a small

Three of Britain's most effective aerial weapons in the Battle of the Atlantic were the Sunderland flying boat (far left), which carried bombs and depth charges and bristled with machine guns, and was dubbed the "flying porcupine" by the Germans; the ancient-looking Swordfish biplane (center), which laid mines, dropped flares and attacked submarines and surface raiders with torpedoes; and the catapult-equipped merchant ship, which carried a Hurricane fighter that strafed U-boats and ships and attacked German aircraft, but could not return to deck once launched.

generator and battery controlled by a hydraulic system originally designed to operate gun turrets. By March 1941, the Leigh Light was undergoing trials and by August it was in production.

The combination of radar and searchlight enabled a plane to make contact at long range, cut its engines and glide silently toward the target, then suddenly illuminate it just before swooping in to attack. Often the first inkling the night deck watch had that his U-boat was being attacked occurred when he saw the chilling glare of the beam—too late to get away.

As the value of air cover began to be appreciated in terms both of U-boats sunk and of ships saved, the Royal Navy began providing convoys with planes of their own to supplement the protection afforded by shore-based aircraft. In the summer of 1941, 50 merchant ships were fitted out with fighter planes that could be catapulted from their bows. These came to be known as Catapult Aircraft Merchantmen, or CAM-ships.

The planes were most useful in fending off the German bombers that continued to plague British shipping in the Western Approaches and in the Bay of Biscay. In August they scored their first sure kill when a Hurricane launched from the catapult-equipped *Maplin* shot down a Focke-Wulf Kondor 400 miles out in the Atlantic.

But the catapult planes were limited in their usefulness. Once they were launched, they could not return to the ship. When his mission was completed, the pilot had to find an airfield—if he was close enough to land—or bail out or ditch his plane close to a friendly ship with the hope that he would be picked up.

A more potent and less hazardous successor to the CAM-ship was a small escort carrier that could carry several planes to sea and receive them again after their missions were over. The earliest of these were converted freighters or passenger liners on which a flight deck and a hangar had been superimposed. Later, the escort carriers were constructed from scratch and became a permanent and vital part of the Royal Navy.

As the fall of 1941 began, Germany had almost 200 commissioned U-boats, 80 of which were in action at any one time, and the numbers were growing. Admiral Dönitz kept probing for weak spots in the convoy traffic—in the areas

south of Greenland and Iceland and northwest of Ireland. Stragglers that fell behind or ships that chose to go it alone were more vulnerable than ever.

When Dönitz chose to tackle a convoy head on, his torpedoes could still take a heavy toll. But the risk was now greater, for the U-boats had to penetrate rings of escort ships that were faster, better armed and more effectively coordinated than they had been in the Happy Time, not many months earlier.

Although more U-boats were operational than ever before, Dönitz suffered from a shortage of highly trained submariners. Most of the prewar captains were dead or captured, or had been promoted to shore assignments. The new generation manning the U-boats lacked not only the experience, but also the sense of invincibility that had spurred their predecessors. Now it was the Allied seamen and their officers who had experience on their side; many had survived the sinking of one or more ships to return to sea. They were also benefiting from the growing number of escort vessels coming down the ways.

Furthermore, the Royal Navy finally had been able to form escort groups in which six or eight small warships trained together and stayed together through several convoy missions. This was a vast improvement over the days when each escort vessel in a convoy was a complete stranger to her neighbor and the captains could barely communicate with each other.

At about the same time this change in policy occurred, the British received a further assist from an unexpected source—Adolf Hitler. The Führer's campaign in North Africa depended on seaborne supplies from Italy and Sicily. But those supplies were being choked off by the British Mediterranean Fleet and by aircraft from the small but indomitable British base at Malta. Hitler pressed Dönitz to divert his submarines from the Atlantic to the Mediterranean—first six boats, then four more; finally, on November 22, came the order to transfer the entire operational force to the Mediterranean and the area west of Gibraltar.

Dönitz, who was steadfast in his belief that the Atlantic was the decisive theater of operations, resisted Hitler's decision for as long as he could. He viewed the Mediterranean as a trap from which his U-boats would never be able to escape. He was right, for not one of the 62 submarines that were stationed in the Mediterranean ever made it back to the Atlantic—although they did score some successes, including the sinking in November of the carrier *Ark Royal* and the battleship *Barham*.

With the switch of the wolf packs to the Mediterranean, shipping losses suddenly declined in the north, while the waters off the coast of Gibraltar became the most dangerous in the world for Allied shipping. The area was heavily trafficked by convoys, some bringing raw materials from the Far East and others carrying war supplies around Africa to the embattled British Eighth Army in Egypt. For nine days in December, the Gibraltar area became the arena of one of the most significant convoy battles of the War, one in which new and highly effective tactics for dealing with the U-boats were introduced. On Sunday afternoon, December 14, Convoy HG-76 sailed out from Gibraltar, a rectangle of 32 merchantmen guarded by two protective rings of warships under Commander F. J. "Johnnie" Walker, a crusty and able antisubmarine tactician who had acquired a reputation for being an outspoken maverick. Walker had been passed over for promotion to captain and had spent the first two years of the War tied to a desk. But he had his own ideas about combating U-boats, and by now he was eager to put them to the test.

In October 1941, Walker had been appointed commanding officer of the sloop *Stork* and named senior officer of an escort group made up of his ship, another sloop and seven corvettes. For two months he worked his team to exhaustion. He drilled them in a series of coordinated battle tactics to which he gave the unlikely name *Buttercup*—a nickname for his wife.

Commander Walker's tactics were designed to bring a maximum number of escort vessels and a maximum amount of firepower to bear against the U-boats at night, when they were most likely to attack. Walker knew that following a successful attack a submarine would either remain near the wreck of the ship that had been torpedoed or make off on the surface at high speed to escape the attention of slower escorts. "Operation *Buttercup*," he explained, "is designed to force the U-boat to dive by plastering the area around the wreck with depth charges and by illuminating the most likely directions of his surface escape. Once submerged, the

Standing astride a pair of depth charges, granite-faced Admiral Sir Percy Noble, Commander-in-Chief, Western Approaches, praises men of the H.M.S. Stork after the sloop sank the U-574. Behind Noble, double row of brass buttons gleaming, is Captain F. J. "Johnnie" Walker, the Stork's commander and the War's top U-boat killer. The Stork dropped depth charges, forcing the U-574 to surface, then rammed and sank her.

destruction of the submarine is considerably simplified."

In early December, Walker's group had escorted the convoy from Liverpool to Gibraltar without incident. But reports from the Submarine Tracking Room in London left no doubt that the run home again could be made only through a savage gauntlet. Submarines already converging toward Gibraltar were being joined by others coming down from the Baltic on Hitler's instructions. A decisive encounter with Dönitz' U-boats was about to occur.

Walker's escort group of nine vessels was augmented by nine Gibraltar-based vessels: three destroyers, two sloops, three corvettes and the escort carrier *Audacity*. But after the first four days, only the *Audacity* and the destroyer *Stanley*, formerly an American four-stacker, would remain with the convoy; the rest of the escort vessels would have to break off and return to Gibraltar. A converted passenger ship that had been captured from the Germans, the *Audacity* was equipped with six small single-seater Grumman Martlet fighter planes.

On the second day out, the brief appearance of a German Kondor bomber on the northern horizon let the convoy know it had been spotted. By evening of the third day, an upsurge in German radio traffic made it ominously clear that a wolf pack was gathering.

Just after 9 a.m. on December 17, the *Audacity*'s planes reported their first sighting: a surfaced U-boat 22 miles on the convoy's port beam. Walker swung five of his ships away in pursuit. A corvette made contact with the now-submerged boat and dropped her depth charges—in patterns of 10 instead of the old limit of five. The submarine *U-131* was forced back to the surface, her hull damaged by the depth charges, but still full of fight. Walker's ships immediately brought the submarine under a blanket of fire from their 4-inch guns. The U-boat's deck gun shot down one of the Martlets, reducing the *Audacity*'s complement to five. But the submarine was fatally damaged, and the captain had no alternative but to abandon her in order to save his crew.

Fine weather the next morning assisted the escort in making its second kill. This time a lookout on the *Stanley* spotted a submarine as she tracked the convoy from six miles off. Within one hour's time, depth charges brought the *U-434* wallowing to the surface. As the escort ships raced up, the submarine turned over and sank, leaving her crew struggling in the water.

So far, the convoy was unscathed as it zigzagged west and north in a wide circle at a speed of seven and a half knots. But now came the time for the remaining Gibraltar-based escort vessels, except the *Stanley,* to peel off for home. And the battle had only begun. Two more Kondors appeared, to assess the position and course of the convoy before the five Martlets chased them off.

At sunset another submarine was sighted, but she got away and the escorts returned to their screen, anticipating a sleepless night. As they did so, the *U-574* shadowed the ships. At 3:45 a.m. the *Stanley,* which was patrolling the rear of the convoy, reported "Submarine in sight." A second message warned: "Torpedoes passing from astern." Commander Walker in the *Stork* was nearest to the *Stanley* and turned to assist her. The two ships were exchanging signals by flashing lights when, with appalling suddenness, the *Stanley* blew up. The *U-574*'s torpedoes had found their mark, setting off an explosion in the *Stanley*'s magazines and splitting the hull of the old destroyer as a sheet of fire shot hundreds of feet into the air.

No sooner had the flames from the *Stanley* died away than the night was lighted up again. All of the merchant ships in the convoy, following standard instructions when a ship was torpedoed, had fired their snowflake rockets. Now everyone—including the assembled U-boats—was able to see the entire area. Moments later a dull thud from the front of the convoy revealed that a submarine had scored another hit on a merchantman.

Meanwhile, Walker raced to the area where the *Stanley* had been hit and was rewarded with a solid asdic contact at short range. The *Stork* blanketed the area twice with depth charges and was turning for a third run when the *U-574* rose to the surface 200 yards ahead. She tried to escape by turning in a tight circle. Walker gave chase; the *Stork*'s turning circle was slightly larger than the U-boat's but her 19-knot speed was just enough to give Walker the edge. He kept closing in and firing his 4-inch guns until they could not be lowered enough to keep the U-boat in their sights. "After this," Walker later wrote in his report of the battle, "the guns' crews were reduced to shaking fists and roaring curses at an enemy who several times seemed to be a matter of a few feet away instead of yards."

The fight had gone on for 11 dizzying minutes, and the U-boat and her pursuer had turned three complete circles, before the *Stork* caught and rammed her. As they scraped apart, a final pattern of depth charges, set to explode at the shallowest depths, finished off the *U-574*.

The *Stanley* had been avenged. But morning brought a warning from the Admiralty that three more U-boats were on their way to join the fight. One of them was commanded by Lieut. Commander Engelbert Endrass, who had been first watch officer on the *U-47* at Scapa Flow and now was the reigning ace of Dönitz' undersea fleet.

There were no new attacks until December 21, the eighth night of the convoy, when a Norwegian tanker went up in flames. Walker ordered a *Buttercup* search to starboard, illuminating the area with snowflakes as the corvettes raced in to sweep the area.

The carrier *Audacity* was 10 miles out, on the starboard flank of the convoy. Her commanding officer was senior to Walker, and he insisted on keeping his ship outside the convoy perimeter. Usually a corvette was detailed to protect her, but tonight none could be spared. The *Audacity* was alone and silhouetted by the glare of snowflakes when a U-boat cautiously approaching the convoy caught sight of her. A torpedo from the submarine hit the *Audacity*'s engine room, flooding it and bringing the carrier to a standstill. The U-boat drew within point-blank range and put two more torpedoes into the carrier. Within 10 minutes the *Audacity* was gone.

For the British the next few hours were a nightmare of submarine sightings, asdic contacts gained and lost and the almost continuous rumble of exploding depth charges. At one point the sloop *Deptford* sighted a submarine inside the perimeter and rushed to the attack. It was Endrass in the *U-567*. The U-boat dived, but the *Deptford* maintained asdic contact and, with assistance from the *Stork,* delivered pattern after pattern of depth charges. The underwater explosions buckled the hull of Endrass' boat and sank her without a trace.

No more ships were torpedoed that night, although the weary British almost managed to sink one of their own vessels. Shortly before dawn the *Deptford* rammed the *Stork* in the darkness. Both ships suffered severe damage.

Meanwhile, the remaining U-boats had drawn off to wait for instructions from headquarters, and in the morning a new element was introduced into the battle. A four-engine Liberator bomber appeared over the convoy. This long-range plane, known in the United States as the B-24, was one of the first of its kind to come into British service and had been assigned to Coastal Command.

The Liberator had flown 800 miles from its base in England to provide air cover for the convoy. In the three hours that it patrolled overhead, it chased off a Kondor and attacked two U-boats that were lying on the surface. One of the submarines had evidently been damaged during the previous night. Her crew scuttled their craft and scrambled to get aboard the other U-boat while the bomber dropped depth charges around them.

The arrival of the Liberator was the last straw for Dönitz, who had been following his commanders' reports on the running battle with increasing dismay. Convoy HG-76 had been under concentrated attack for a week, and had lost only two of its 32 ships. The cost to the Germans had been five U-boats out of the total of nine that Dönitz had committed to the battle, including the submarine that was commanded by Endrass, who was the most experienced of his remaining captains.

Dönitz ordered his U-boats to abandon the attack against the convoy. Given port-to-port air cover and the kind of scrappy escort that Johnnie Walker had thrown up around HG-76, British convoys were proving too much for the U-boat fleet. In a showdown between submarines and a determined, well-escorted convoy, the submarine had been decisively defeated.

The U-boats needed easier hunting than they were encountering in the Gibraltar area and in the North Atlantic, and Dönitz knew just where to look for it. On December 7, Japan had bombed Pearl Harbor and four days later Germany had joined her Axis partner at war with the United States. With America in the scrap at last, the vast flow of unprotected shipping from the Gulf of Mexico up the Eastern Seaboard of North America as far as Nova Scotia was now fair game for the submarines. In 1942 they turned their attention to it with a vengeance.

AMERICA'S ICY CITADEL

British and American warships assemble in Iceland's sprawling Hvalfjordur harbor before starting out with a convoy for the Russian port of Archangel.

THE BATTLE AGAINST BOREDOM

"Whoever possesses Iceland," wrote the German geopolitician Karl Haushofer in the 1930s, "holds a pistol pointed permanently at England, America and Canada." It was a pistol that Great Britain was quick to seize. In May 1940, with the fall of Denmark, the island's former ruler, Britain raced to take control of this subarctic outpost that lay within easy reach of vital shipping routes, putting ashore a force that soon swelled to more than 24,000 men. But a little more than a year later, when the British troops there were needed for duty in Africa, all but a few were gradually pulled out and American Marines took over—a full five months before the United States formally became involved in the War. Eventually as many as 50,000 Americans were stationed there.

The U.S. defenders of Iceland found themselves in a bleak realm. At the height of winter in the far northern latitudes, daylight lasted only four hours. Gale force winds buffeted men and machines. Heavy rains could transform camps into quagmires. With the weather in mind, the Army issued every GI skis and snowshoes—and an unheard-of five pairs of shoes.

Monotony was the No. 1 enemy, more real to most servicemen than the Germans. Some men flew routine air patrols or patched up damaged ships, but the chief excitement available to most of them was training, building roads, erecting huts or hauling supplies. There were few diversions afterhours, except for letters home, card games or reading. The local girls were none too friendly, the beer was weak, and Scotch cost a dollar a shot—a lot of money in the days when a buck private got only $30 a month.

The Americans made the most of their surroundings. They did their laundry in natural hot springs that bubbled up out of Iceland's volcanic terrain, and paved the streets around camp with crushed lava to combat the mud. And as an indication that they had not lost their sense of humor, they fashioned trees out of empty cans and discarded pipes to decorate the barren landscape, built wooden fireplugs and put up street signs bearing familiar hometown names.

Iceland changes command in 1942 as U.S. Major General Charles Bonesteel (second from left) takes over from British Major-General H. O. Curtis.

On lonely, frigid guard duty in March 1943, a U.S. Marine, shouldering a bayonet-tipped Garand rifle, keeps watch at Fleet Air Base in Reykjavik.

Wearing hip boots, an American soldier struggles to lay a walkway of discarded cans through the muddy morass surrounding a busy corner at Jeffersonville Camp, near Reykjavik. Semicylindrical Nissen huts like this one were warmed by pot-bellied stoves and housed a dozen men.

With precision cadence, crack troops of the 10th U.S. Infantry Regiment march by Nissen huts lining one of Iceland's wet and treeless roads. The huts were widely used in the War, but were especially well adapted to Iceland: they had no seams for wind to penetrate, no eaves for the wind to rattle, no crannies in which snow could gather. An air space underneath the floorboards helped to insulate the interiors.

American sailors bend to the task of clearing snow off the flight deck of the visiting carrier U.S.S. Wasp. The newly commissioned warship was caught in a snowstorm after delivering 30 Army Air Corps P-40 fighters sent from America to bolster Iceland's air defense.

Remnants of two PBM Mariner flying boats, sunk at Reykjavik by a 120-mph gale, lie on the shore.

A seaman grabs for support as waves break over the middle of a tanker (background) at Hvalfjordur.

Prior to takeoff for convoy-escort duty, two U.S. Navy patrol pilots study a grid chart in their squadron headquarters at Reykjavik showing them where they should rendezvous with a convoy approaching Iceland. Air coverage of convoys started 600 miles out, with patrol planes taking turns at escorting the vessels in four-hour shifts.

PBY Catalinas of a U.S. Navy patrol squadron return from a reconnaissance mission. The amphibious "Cats" bucked gales and rain squalls to comb the waters for U-boats and deadly ice. They also conducted searches for planes downed in the sea and for survivors of ship sinkings.

A jagged incision in the bow of the merchant ship S.S. Exford—framed with scaffolding for repairs in Hvalfjordur harbor—attests to the destruction that sea ice could inflict even on steel plate. Off the coast of Iceland, icebergs that had broken off from the arctic pack and floated into convoy lanes imperiled shipping during the spring and summer months.

Crippled by a German torpedo almost two months before America entered the War, the U.S.S. Kearny (right) undergoes repairs next to the repair ship Vulcan in Hvalfjordur. The Kearny was hit after going to the aid of a convoy that had been attacked by a U-boat wolf pack. She suffered 11 dead, the United States' first military casualties of the War.

Standing solemnly at attention as wreaths are placed on graves, British and American servicemen stationed in Iceland pay a final tribute to victims of

the Battle of the Atlantic during a Memorial Day service held in 1943. Before the end of the War, some 450 Allied casualties were laid to rest there.

6

American neutrality under fire
The U.S. backs into war
Trading American ships for British bases
Churchill lays it on the line
Lend-Lease: "An ocean-borne trumpet call"
The Allied leaders meet
A Presidential order to shoot on sight
The first American ship goes down
The U-boats invade U.S. coastal waters
Bucket-brigade convoys
A costly blunder in the Arctic

American participation in the Battle of the Atlantic long predated the nation's official entry into the War. United States involvement traced back, in fact, to September 3, 1939, the day Britain and France declared war on Germany. That evening President Franklin D. Roosevelt addressed the nation by radio. With his customary air of a paterfamilias, the President spoke in measured cadence: "Passionately though we may desire detachment, we are forced to realize that every word that comes through the air, every ship that sails the sea, every battle that is fought, does affect the American future."

He did not suggest how America's future might be affected, nor how Americans should think about the War. But his peroration left no doubt that he expected them to do some heavy thinking about what side they were on. "This nation will remain a neutral nation," he said, "but I cannot ask that every American remain neutral in thought as well. Even a neutral has a right to take account of facts. Even a neutral cannot be asked to close his mind or his conscience."

It soon became evident that Roosevelt's own sympathies—and, as it turned out, those of most of his constituents—lay with the Allies. In the two years that followed his speech, American attention focused on the Atlantic—and on the British waging their lone fight there. By December 1941, when the United States and Germany formally went to war, the Americans had begun to send great stores of weapons and supplies across the ocean to Britain. American ships had been sunk, and many Americans had died in an attempt to keep Britain's lifeline open.

But surprisingly, when America finally became an active belligerent, the Battle of the Atlantic—just as the British seemed at last to be getting the upper hand—actually took a turn for the worse.

The first step in the process of changing America's status from that of onlooker to active participant occurred that same first month of the War, when Roosevelt dispatched Under Secretary of State Sumner Welles to a conference in Panama in an effort to win Latin America's cooperation in keeping the Western Hemisphere neutral. The outcome was the Declaration of Panama, in which the United States and the Latin American republics joined together in proclaiming the waters extending 300 miles off the United States

THE UNITED STATES AT SEA

and South American coasts to be a neutral zone, and ordering the belligerent powers to keep out—in effect, a warning to Germany. To enforce the declaration, Roosevelt ordered the U.S. Navy to set up a so-called Neutrality Patrol of 80 destroyers to operate in this zone.

The second step required subtler political skill and a greater measure of perseverance. Roosevelt moved to persuade Congress to reverse the laws that prevented the U.S. from helping Britain and France.

The Neutrality Act, first passed in 1935 and later renewed, reflected the lingering disillusionment of Americans with World War I, and an attempt to isolate the United States from foreign conflicts. It forbade American ships to carry freight or passengers to the ports of belligerent nations, and empowered the President to declare combat zones that were out of bounds for American ships. It also prohibited the arming of American merchant ships and outlawed the sale of arms to belligerent nations—though raw materials could be sold if the purchasing nations paid cash, and picked up and ferried their purchases home.

Roosevelt's effort to get the Neutrality Act amended encountered bitter opposition from the start. "We need the neutrality law. We need restraints upon a President," said isolationist Senator Gerald P. Nye of North Dakota.

But Roosevelt and his adherents had a compelling argument: Britain and France had several billion dollars' worth of planes on order from American factories. As the Neutrality Act then stood, these friendly powers would not be able to come and fetch their planes, although they critically needed them and other equipment to prosecute the War.

By deft courting of nonpartisan sentiment and timely compromise, the President secured the passage of a new Neutrality Act in November 1939, two months after the outbreak of war in Europe. The new law retained most of the provisions of the previous law but permitted the sale of arms—as well as raw materials—to belligerents on a cash-and-carry basis. Ostensibly, any country could buy these arms, but the amendment clearly favored Britain and France, for the British blockade of Germany kept German ships from crossing the Atlantic to pick up weapons.

From now on, Roosevelt's basic approach was to do as much as he could for Great Britain and France without incurring the wrath of American isolationists on the one hand, or driving Hitler to a declaration of war on the other.

On May 15, 1940, in a move that was as novel as it was brash, Prime Minister Winston Churchill capitalized on a growing friendship with the President and asked for an outright gift of American destroyers—the four-stackers left over from World War I—"to bridge the gap between what we have now and the large new construction we put in hand at the beginning of the war."

The proposal was viewed as a trap by isolationists. "If we want to get into war," protested the *Chicago Tribune,* "the destroyers offer as good a way as any." What appeared to be a stripping of the American arsenal also caused deep concern in some quarters; moreover, many Americans felt that, given the present rate of ship sinkings in the Atlantic—and given Britain's dire predicament at this point—handing the destroyers over to Britain would be tantamount to turning them over to Germany. Congress sought to defuse the issue by stipulating that only such war matériel as could be certified unnecessary to American defense would be sold or otherwise disposed of.

On June 10, with German victory in France clearly imminent, Roosevelt used the graduation ceremonies at the University of Virginia as a forum in which he proposed giving "the opponents of force" the full benefit of America's material resources—a policy that came to be characterized as "all aid short of war." Churchill soon renewed his urgent plea to Roosevelt for American destroyers. "Mr. President," he wrote, "with great respect I must tell you that in the long history of the world this is a thing to do *now.*"

At that point a group of prominent American businessmen, lawyers and intellectuals belonging to the prestigious Century Group, a political action club, came up with a solution to the problem of the destroyers. Ironically, the idea evolved out of an old isolationist scheme. The *Chicago Tribune* had long advocated the turning over of British bases in the Western Hemisphere to the United States in exchange for unpaid World War I debts. The Century Group, adapting the idea to the current situation, proposed that the British relinquish their West Indies bases for the destroyers they needed.

The suggestion broke the logjam. On September 2, 1940, Secretary of State Cordell Hull and British Ambassador Lord Lothian signed an agreement by which the destroyers were to go to Britain in exchange for 99-year leases on six bases: on Great Exuma Island in the Bahamas, on Jamaica, Antigua, St. Lucia, Trinidad and in British Guiana. As a bonus—not technically part of the destroyer exchange—the British threw in bases on Bermuda and in Newfoundland. On the 4th of September the first of the 50 destroyers—many had been mothballed in the Philadelphia Navy Yard since World War I—were refitted and steamed out of Boston for Halifax in Nova Scotia. From there, the Royal Navy took them over.

The sudden enlargement of their fleet by 50 destroyers gave the British immediate reason for hope, but their spirits were dashed in the autumn, when Germany's ferocious effort to knock out British cities from the air went into high gear. By November, British officials were desperately pleading for some two billion dollars' worth of American munitions, although by now they had no money to pay for them. With extraordinary frankness, Churchill laid bare to Roosevelt Britain's needs: 7,000 combat aircraft, 7,000 training planes and three million tons of merchant ships plus assorted weaponry. He did not tally up the cost, but together all this matériel would come to a staggering five billion dollars.

Roosevelt was in a very difficult position. On November 5 of that year he had been re-elected to an unprecedented third term. He had weathered the political storms that had been stirred up not only by the destroyer deal but also by the first peacetime draft of U.S. forces in history. But it had been the closest victory of his Presidential career. Could he risk another showdown with Congress so soon afterward?

On December 2, Roosevelt went off on one of his favorite recreations—a fishing cruise—"as carefree as you please," wrote his biographer Robert Sherwood, and seeming for all the world to have lost interest in the War. "That, however, was only as it seemed," Sherwood added.

The problem of aid to Britain was solved after the President returned—healthily tanned and in high spirits. One day, lunching with Treasury Secretary Henry Morgenthau Jr., Roosevelt had what Morgenthau called "one of the President's brilliant flashes."

Their discussion, centering around Britain's financial dilemma, appeared to be foundering when Roosevelt suddenly said, "It seems to me the thing to do is to get away from the dollar sign. I don't want to put the thing in terms of dollars or loans." Then he came to the point: "We will say to England, 'We will give you the guns and ships you need, provided that when the war is over you will return to us in kind the guns and ships we have loaned you.'" If military bases could be leased for eventual return—as they had been under the terms of the destroyer deal—why not planes and guns?

The President was introducing the revolutionary concept that came to be known as Lend-Lease, but his offhand manner cloaked the gravity of the idea he had just proposed. At a press conference that afternoon, he amplified the idea with one of the homely analogies he loved to use when addressing the American public. "Suppose my neighbor's home catches fire and I have a length of garden hose," he said. "I don't say to him: 'Neighbor, my garden hose cost me $15; you have to pay me $15 for it.' No! I don't want $15—I want my garden hose back after the fire is over." So it would be with the fire in Britain.

Events were now proceeding at an ever-quickening pace. In January 1941, the Joint Chiefs of Staff began meeting with their British counterparts; they eventually settled on the so-called ABC-1 Staff Agreement, by which both nations were pledged—in the event of worldwide conflagration—to dispose of Germany first, no matter what might happen elsewhere. In February the United States Navy's Neutrality Patrol was renamed the United States Atlantic Fleet.

On the 11th of March, Congress passed the Lend-Lease Bill. In retrospect it ranks among the turning points of World War II. According to its terms, Britain was to receive seven billion dollars' worth of American equipment by June 30, 1942. In effect, half of America's mighty economic and manufacturing assets were placed at the disposal of the British in their fight against the Axis. Churchill expressed his relief with his customary eloquence. "The words and acts of the President and the people of the United States," he said, "come to us like a draft of life, and they tell us by an ocean-borne trumpet call that we are no longer alone."

One month later the United States quietly assumed a protectorate over the Danish-owned territory of Greenland, and routed some German detachments that were manning weather stations there.

By May, the number of sinkings by U-boats in the Atlantic had risen alarmingly, to a rate that was more than three times the capacity of British shipyards to replace, and more than twice the combined British and American output. The sinkings were beginning to have a special relevance for Americans. A recent casualty, the Egyptian steamer *Zamzam (pages 24-37),* had scores of American passengers on board when she was attacked by a German surface raider in the South Atlantic. Moreover, the first consignments of Lend-Lease goods soon were to set sail for England.

On May 27, seizing on the dangers that were creeping closer and closer to American interests, the President proclaimed the existence of an "unlimited national emergen-

Mothballed World War I destroyers jam the Philadelphia Navy Yard prior to being exchanged in September 1940 for British bases in the West Indies and British Guiana. Forty-four of the four-stackers were turned over to Britain and six were delivered to Canada. Above, Canadian officers in Halifax, Nova Scotia, march to take over one of the destroyers that will be used for escorting convoys traveling in the North Atlantic.

cy," and announced that he was extending naval patrols deeper into the North and South Atlantic. American ships in those waters were under orders to keep a wary eye out for German ships, but not to shoot. Americans, now far from resisting the new defense measures, were beginning to clamor for more effective action. "I hope that we will protect every dollar's worth of stuff that we send to Great Britain, and that we will shoot the hell out of anybody who interferes," said Virginia's crusty Senator Carter Glass.

By this time Churchill and Roosevelt had developed an easy camaraderie—but only through correspondence. They had crossed paths at a dinner in London nearly a quarter century before, when Roosevelt was Assistant Secretary of the Navy and Churchill a British Cabinet member, but as chiefs of state they had not met. Both were eager to get to know each other firsthand. "I have just got to see Churchill myself in order to explain things to him," Roosevelt once

said to Secretary Morgenthau. Churchill, speaking to Averell Harriman, the President's special representative for Lend-Lease in Britain, remarked: "I wonder if he will like me?"

A meeting was arranged at Argentia, a secluded port in the Bay of Placentia on the coast of Newfoundland. To get there, Churchill had to make a risky crossing through waters where U-boats lurked. The preparations took place in greatest secrecy on both sides—and with some subterfuge on the American side that fooled even the Secret Service.

Roosevelt set sail from New London, Connecticut, on August 3, 1941. Ostensibly he was off on a pleasure cruise on the Presidential yacht *Potomac,* to do some deep-sea fishing in the congenial company of his doctor and two White House aides. Once at sea, Roosevelt secretly boarded the cruiser *Augusta* and headed for Newfoundland, while the *Potomac* set a course through the Cape Cod Canal, where crowds of vacationers had gathered along the shore

Prime Minister Winston Churchill and President Franklin D. Roosevelt take time out from drafting the Atlantic Charter aboard the U.S.S. Augusta to be photographed with their staffs—and the President's Scottie, Fala, seated at his feet. At a dinner hosted by Roosevelt, Churchill made an eloquent address, calling for a sea blockade of Europe, subversion and strategic bombing as the keys to victory over Germany.

to catch a glimpse of the eminent fisherman. What they glimpsed—without being any the wiser—were members of the yacht's crew, lolling conspicuously on the deck, dressed in white ducks. One of the men was obligingly nodding and waving with Presidential benevolence.

Six days later the real Presidential party rendezvoused in Newfoundland with the H.M.S. *Prince of Wales* and her passengers, the Prime Minister and his entourage. The two leaders promptly got down to business, conferring in pri-

vate and in the company of their highest ranking state and military chiefs. Because of the crippled President's difficulty in moving about, the Prime Minister made the graceful gesture of going to the President's ship for most of their meetings. But on Sunday, Roosevelt went aboard the *Prince of Wales* for religious services. Churchill received his distinguished guest with a gallant display of seamanly expertise. When the destroyer ferrying the President pulled alongside the *Prince of Wales,* the Prime Minister stood alone on the battleship's fantail and personally helped haul in the line that secured the two ships together.

The public learned about the historic meeting in the form of a press release whose text has endured under the name of the Atlantic Charter, a statement of elegant simplicity and intentional vagueness designed to set forth the objectives of the two nations. In the name of the British and American people, it declared that they sought no territorial gains from the War; that peoples everywhere should be free to choose their own forms of government; that all peoples should be entitled to trade freely, with the goal of better standards of living for all; and that all peoples must abandon force as a means of solving international differences.

What the public was not told was that Roosevelt and Churchill had also reached some specific agreements on more immediate issues. Paramount among these was the matter of safe delivery of Lend-Lease goods to England— and now to Russia as well, since Germany had invaded the Soviet Union on June 22. Roosevelt took the bold step of pledging that warships of the U.S. Navy would escort British merchant ships as far as Iceland, where U.S. Marines had recently landed to relieve the British of the task of occupying this vital North Atlantic outpost *(pages 134-147).*

America's progress toward direct participation in the War was soon accelerated by a series of incidents that took place in the Greenland-Iceland area. On the 4th of September, southwest of Iceland, a submarine exchanged fire with the American destroyer *Greer.* Who was guilty of provoking whom was open to question, but Roosevelt capitalized on the episode. "Let this warning be clear," he announced. "From now on if German or Italian vessels enter the waters the protection of which is necessary for American defense, they do so at their own peril." Ameri-

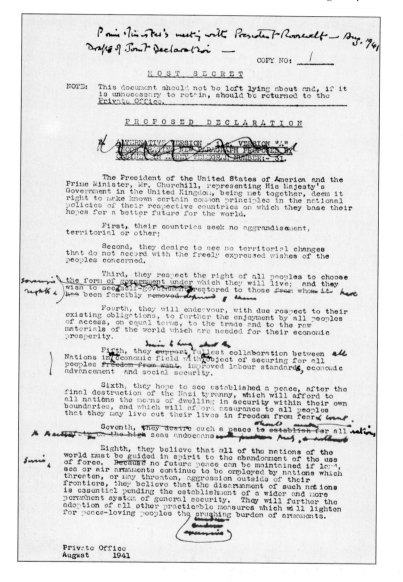

The first draft of the Atlantic Charter was written by Churchill after extensive discussion with Roosevelt. Paragraphs six and seven were contributed by the President. Churchill's editing is scrawled illegibly in red ink. The document affirmed the two nations' commitment to the "final destruction of Nazi tyranny," although at this point—August 1941—the United States still was not at war with Germany.

can ships henceforth were under orders to shoot on sight.

The American public accepted the new state of affairs in a somber mood. Many people began to clamor for better protection for the ships, and pressure mounted for repeal of the Neutrality Act, which was once again being debated in Congress.

While the debate occupied Capitol Hill, two more incidents occurred to color public opinion. On October 17 the U.S. destroyer *Kearny* was torpedoed with the loss of 11 men while defending a beleaguered British convoy off Iceland. The *Kearny* limped safely into port, but on October 27, Navy Day, Roosevelt used the incident to gain support for his international policy. "America has been attacked," he said. "The U.S.S. *Kearny* is not just a Navy ship. She belongs to every man, woman and child in this nation." On October 31 another U.S. destroyer, the *Reuben James*, was sunk while escorting a convoy eastbound from Halifax. It was the first sinking of an American ship in the Battle of the Atlantic, and casualties were high: 115.

In mid-November, Congress passed further amendments to the Neutrality Act. The body of the old law remained, but some important restrictions were relaxed. American ships were permitted now to sail into belligerent ports; American warships were free to escort convoys into the war zone, thus relieving British ships needed for duty elsewhere; and American merchant ships were allowed to be armed.

Only three weeks remained before the Japanese attack on Pearl Harbor and the formal U.S. declaration of war. But by now the United States already was deeply enmeshed in the Atlantic combat zone.

U.S. entry into the War brought a swift reaction in the Atlantic. Admiral Dönitz mounted a full-scale attack along America's East Coast—an area vital to U.S. shipping and one that afforded an irresistible opportunity for his U-boats.

The assault, given the code name of *Drum Roll,* was launched in January. Perhaps its most surprising aspect was the small number of submarines involved. At the beginning of 1942, Dönitz had 91 U-boats at his disposal. Twenty-three were in the Mediterranean—under orders from Hitler and Grand Admiral Raeder to attack Allied ships supplying British forces in the Egyptian desert—and three more were on their way to that area. Six U-boats were positioned west of Gibraltar, and four more were hovering off Norway. That left Dönitz only 55 subs for Atlantic duty, and at that time 60 per cent of them were in drydock for repairs. Thus, only 22 U-boats were active in the Atlantic—and approximately half of these were traveling to or from the combat zones.

But with those dozen or so U-boats Dönitz achieved staggering results.

The submarine crews set off for the new war zone "in fine spirits," Dönitz later wrote, "taking with them high hopes such as we at U-boat Command had not had for many a day." There were no convoys off the American coast, no escorts to contend with—just single ships plying the regular shipping routes. The subs simply strung themselves out along the coast from New England to northern Florida and attacked at will. The first hit was scored on January 12 against the *Cyclops,* a British passenger ship that sank off Cape Cod, with 87 lives lost. In the 19 days remaining in January, the U-boats sank 13 more vessels totaling 95,000 tons. In the next four months they took a terrible toll. Of the 441 Allied merchant ships lost to the submarines between January and the end of May, 87 were sunk in American waters. More than half of the loss was in tankers, most of them carrying the War's lifeblood, oil.

The new offensive took Americans by surprise. Yet they did almost nothing to minimize its effects. Every day thousands of tons of irreplaceable cargo sailed, unescorted, up the coast. No instructions were given the captains as to what to do in the event of U-boat attack. None of the planes that could fly far out to sea were on hand to do so—and few American pilots knew how to deal effectively with a U-boat if they spotted one. Moreover, when the first bumbling efforts got under way to meet these deficiencies, no single authority existed to coordinate them properly.

Worst, perhaps, the American ships were conspicuous —and careless. Their personnel were both inexperienced and gullible. Ships' crews talked to each other on their radios, providing vital information to the lurking U-boats. One submarine commander, spying a freighter in the light of a tanker the U-boat had just set ablaze, signaled: "This is the lightship. You are standing into danger. Direct your course to pass close to me." The freighter immediately obeyed—and was torpedoed and sunk, losing 20 men.

Ashore, cities resisted blackouts. Miami sported a six-mile

strip of neon that silhouetted ships by night, but the Chamber of Commerce refused to douse the lights lest such a move scare the tourists away. The tourists gathered on the beaches to watch torpedoed ships blazing on the horizon.

Naval authorities often were as perverse as the tourists. To the despair of the British, who—after more than two years of painful trial and error in what one American admiral aptly described as the "laboratory of war"—had virtually driven the U-boats from their coasts, the U.S. resisted all manner of British advice. The Americans were even loath to adopt the tried-and-true convoy system along the Eastern Seaboard. The Navy believed that a weakly escorted convoy was worse than a convoy with no protection at all; contending that it lacked enough ships for proper escorts, it provided none. Most American naval vessels capable of coping with U-boats had already gone north to shepherd convoys on the all-important North Atlantic run from Halifax to Iceland—which were now carrying troops as well as cargo. The remainder were on duty in the Pacific, trying to fend off the Japanese, who were advancing through the Philippines and Southeast Asia.

With all these far-flung commitments, there were only about two dozen vessels in the U.S. Navy available to cover the Eastern Sea Frontier—the official designation for the

THE INFAMOUS LACONIA INCIDENT

On the 12th of September, 1942, the British troopship Laconia, a 19,965-ton converted ocean liner, was torpedoed in the South Atlantic by the U-156, commanded by Werner Hartenstein. The 2,732 passengers on the ship included 1,800 Italians captured in North Africa, and the families of British colonial civil servants. Hearing cries for help in Italian, and fearing a great loss of life in shark-infested waters, Hartenstein sought to rescue the survivors.

The Laconia had already broadcast a distress signal, but Hartenstein augmented it with English broadcasts asking all ships in the area for help. He also notified Admiral Dönitz, who radioed the U-506 and the U-507 to join in the rescue. Vichy French authorities in Dakar dispatched the cruiser Gloire and two smaller ships.

Meanwhile, Hartenstein rescued 260 survivors, later transferring half to the U-506. Another 157 were brought on board the U-507, and scores more were placed in lifeboats. The decks of the U-boats were full and the crowded lifeboats were in tow when an American Liberator bomber appeared, circled and departed. A half hour later the Liberator returned and dropped five bombs on Hartenstein's U-boat, ignoring flashing signals, radio messages and a Red Cross flag. (The pilot's later explanation for the attack was that two other Allied ships were in the area and were endangered by the U-boats' presence.)

The U-156 was damaged and Hartenstein was forced to return his survivors to the water. Nevertheless, Dönitz ordered the other two U-boats to continue rescue operations. On September 18, the submarines rendezvoused with the French ships and 1,200 persons were saved.

As a result of the Liberator's attack, Dönitz ordered all U-boats henceforth not to rescue survivors. In the Nuremberg trial after the War, he was charged with murder for giving this order. Although the tribunal convicted Dönitz of other war crimes, he was acquitted on the murder charge, on the ground that the Allies themselves had waged unrestricted submarine warfare and had rarely rescued survivors.

The sleek Cunard White Star liner Laconia was the second ship to bear the name. The first one was torpedoed by the Germans during World War I.

280,000-square-mile ocean area between the Bay of Fundy and Jacksonville. To use those two dozen ships for escort duty, the Navy argued, would leave such vital harbors as New York, Boston, Norfolk and Charleston unprotected. "The plain fact of the matter is that we have not the 'tools' wherewith to meet the enemy at all the points he is threatening," wrote Admiral Ernest J. King, commander in chief of the U.S. Navy, to a colleague. "All in all, we have to do the best we can with what we've got."

Holding fast to that conviction, the Navy attempted to meet the U-boat menace with hunting patrols—a practice long since discarded by the British. "This is one of the hardest of all the lessons of war to swallow," an Admiralty report noted in an attempt to dissuade the U.S. Navy from pursuing this fruitless tactic. "To go to sea to hunt down and destroy the enemy makes a strong appeal to every naval officer," it added. "It gives a sense of the offensive that is lacking in the more humdrum business of convoy protection. But in this U-boat war, the limitations of hunting forces have made themselves very clear."

Like an adolescent bent on showing his independence of the irksome voice of experience, the U.S. Navy refused to listen. And its persistence in sending out hunting patrols was welcomed by the Germans. "It did not take the U-boats long to work out a very effective routine," Dönitz wrote. "By day they lay on the bottom at depths of anything from 150 to 450 feet and a few miles away from the shipping routes. At dusk they approached the coast submerged and when darkness fell surfaced in the middle of a stream of shipping to deliver their attacks by night." The eager U.S. hunting patrols did not manage to sight, much less put out of commission, a single U-boat until April 14—three full months after the submarines' arrival along the coast.

While the hunting patrols were failing, the U.S. was trying a number of other tactics that the British had also tried and discarded. One was the fabrication of five "Mystery Ships," or Q-ships. Armed merchant ships, their weapons concealed by netting, masqueraded as innocent freighters and trawlers. On sighting a U-boat the Q-ship would fling off her disguise and fire away. The first three Q-ships set out from the New England coast in March 1942. Four days later, a U-boat sank one of them—costing the lives of 148 men. After more than a year, the Q-ships' total achievement was

three encounters with U-boats—all of which got away.

Another fruitless scheme was to enlist the aid of commercial fishermen. The idea was the brain child of Commander Vincent Astor, a yachting enthusiast and member of the Naval Reserve. With Navy blessing, he outfitted fishermen from Maine to Florida with two-way radios, and bade them report anything suspicious. But fishermen are an independent lot, accustomed to taking their own good time. When they found the presence of unfamiliar craft worthy of comment at all, they frequently waited so long to convey the intelligence that the submarines had vanished.

Meanwhile, the Germans pressed their attack without let-up, aided by an innovation they called the "milch cow." This was a lumbering 1,600-ton U-boat, serving as a mobile storehouse that on a single voyage could supply U-boats with food, spare parts and fuel, thereby doubling from two weeks to four the time each U-boat could remain at sea.

By March the Admiralty was on the point of losing patience. Critical supplies destined for Britain via the U.S. coastal route were not getting through. In an effort to convince the Americans of the importance of adopting convoy formations, the British proposed to send 10 corvettes and two dozen antisubmarine trawlers from their own shipyards, together with a pair of experienced officers who would teach the American novices how to use the escorts to best advantage against the U-boats. The U.S. Navy turned down the offer of personnel, preferring to do things its own way.

The Navy did accept the ships, however—putting them to work on April 1, 1942, in a partial convoy system that was soon to be dubbed the "bucket brigade." Under this system, merchant ships received escort protection by day during 120-mile dashes between harbors such as Jacksonville and Charleston; they then laid over in safe anchorages by night. It was a modest beginning, but a step in the right direction. By May that system had evolved into a proper convoy operation between New York and Halifax, and between Key West and Norfolk. By July it had become an interlocking convoy system extending all the way from the oil-rich Dutch island of Aruba, off the northern coast of South America, to Halifax. Like passengers boarding or leaving a train at a local railroad station, merchant ships could join or leave a convoy at any port along the way. They passed by relay from one escort group to another as they left one port and headed for the next.

Together with beefed-up air coverage, the tardily instituted convoy system yielded dramatic results. Sinkings dropped from 23 in April to five in May, and to zero in July. But by then the U-boats had already caused havoc: in six months more than half a million tons of shipping had been sent to the bottom of the ocean off the American coast.

In the spring and summer of 1942, as the number of sinkings on the Eastern Sea Frontier decreased, the U-boats moved to other killing grounds. They found a fruitful one off the Arctic coast of Russia—along the forbidding route taken by the convoys relaying Lend-Lease goods to the Soviet Union. In this new German offensive, American ships—sailing under British command—were to witness the full fury of war at sea, a fury compounded by some maladroit planning by Allied commanders in the face of enemy tactics.

From high quarters to low, everyone viewed the Russian convoy run with suspicion, distaste or dread. Sailors called it "hell below zero"; even in summer there could be temperatures below freezing and rough seas. Admiral Sir Dudley Pound, Britain's First Sea Lord, called it a "millstone round our necks." With the lengthening days in the far north, casualties rose. In one convoy in mid-March, five out of 19 merchant ships were sunk. And among the spring casualties were two cruisers Britain could ill afford to lose.

Meanwhile, the Admiralty had another worry. British intelligence reported that the Germans had removed several of their big warships—of which the most formidable was the brand-new, 42,500-ton battleship Tirpitz—from home base in Germany and berthed them on the Norwegian coast, only a few days' sail from the Arctic convoy route. These warships were supplemented by Luftwaffe planes, also now based in Norway, as well as by the ubiquitous U-boats. Because of the danger, the Admiralty began urging the British government to discontinue the Arctic run at least until fall, when the long nights would return.

But the government had other concerns. Germany had by this time committed 80 per cent of its land forces to the Russian invasion, and Russia was fighting for its life. To Churchill and Roosevelt, the need to sustain the Soviet Union was urgent. They could spare no troops to help the country in its ordeal, but they could contribute war goods—and had promised to do so.

And so the convoys continued into June, with their casualties growing increasingly worse. These reached a culmination with PQ-17, the 17th convoy to leave Iceland for Russia. The PQ-17 journey turned into a debacle that Churchill was later to call "one of the most melancholy naval episodes in the whole of the war."

PQ-17 originated in Hvalfjordur, Iceland, on June 27, 1942, bound for Archangel, Russia. It consisted of 35 merchant ships—22 of them American—carrying $700 million worth of planes, tanks, guns and other war matériel; also along were three rescue ships and two tankers. That was an unusually large convoy, and it had an even larger number of ships to protect it—47 in all. There was a close escort of 21 ships, all British, and including two submarines. There was also a supporting force, which was to travel the convoy's route but remain out of sight. This consisted of seven ships: four cruisers—two of them American—and three destroyers. Finally, there was also a distant covering force of 19 warships that included two battleships, one of them American, and one British aircraft carrier, the Victorious; these were patrolling the waters between Iceland and Norway, and were expected to be ready to intercept the Tirpitz if she left port.

To the men who were charged with carrying out the mission, such an assemblage obviously meant something important was afoot, and although they knew nothing of the arguments over the political and naval strategy taking place in high quarters, they shared a growing apprehension. Remembering the grim-faced skippers of the escort ships as they awaited orders to sail, Commander John E. Broome of the British destroyer Keppel, who was in charge of the close escort, wrote: "They were seamen, they knew jolly well that this floating town they were about to form would fill some 25 miles of nonstop visibility. They hadn't got to be told that enemy U-boats, and planes and warships would take advantage of this."

Once the convoy got under way, misgivings eased for a time. The ships were veiled in welcome fog, and the first four days went by with no sign of the enemy. Three ships had to turn back to port, but not because of attack; one ran aground on the rocks off Iceland and two were damaged by heavy ice floes. Then on July 1 a solitary German plane appeared aloft, "its nose tipped slightly to the water, like some ominous nose-to-sea bloodhound," one British officer later recalled. Tension mounted again. Commander Broome wrote that it "brought a chilly feeling knowing that from now on, visibility permitting, PQ-17 would be plotted on German operational wall maps as well as our own."

The next few days brought sporadic raids from the air, but no damage until early on July 4, when a Heinkel-115 torpedo bomber hit one of the ships; a U-boat finished her off. As the day wore on the air raids subsided, and British ships were astonished to find the American ships lowering their tattered ensigns as if in surrender—only to raise spanking clean Stars and Stripes instead; then the U.S. sailors began to celebrate the Fourth of July with singing and dancing on deck. The British ships joined into the spirit of the occasion; the British cruiser *Norfolk* signaled the American cruiser *Wichita:* "Many happy returns of the day. The United States is the only country with a known birthday." And the *Wichita*, enjoying some comic relief of her own, responded, "We think you should celebrate Mother's Day."

In the evening came a new attack by 25 German planes.

Crewmen paint the American merchantman S.S. Troubadour white to camouflage her from German aircraft after convoy PQ-17, to which she belonged, was ordered to scatter on the Arctic run to Russia in July 1942. With three other ships, she hid among the ice floes three days, blending with the background, until she could proceed to Archangel.

Three were shot down, but three merchant ships were hit—two so badly damaged they had to be sunk. But spirits remained high in the knowledge that the halfway point to Archangel had been reached.

Back in London the Admiralty was enjoying no such high spirits. Unknown to all but a few escort officers, British officials had learned that the *Tirpitz* had eluded surveillance; she was known to be somewhere at sea, and was thought to be heading east, in the direction of the convoy, together with several other German warships. Looking back, it would appear that the Admiralty panicked; in any event, it concluded that the *Tirpitz* and the other German warships were closing in on the convoy, and sent out to the startled escort vessels some new and unexpected orders. Three excited messages came over the wireless in the space of 25 minutes. The first ordered the supporting cruiser force to turn back westward. The second ordered the convoy to disperse and proceed individually to Archangel. The last and fatal message was: "Convoy is to scatter." This meant that the merchant ships were to fan out in all directions.

On the escort ships, officers and men alike were stunned. One of the officers aboard the *Wichita,* actor Douglas Fairbanks Jr., recorded the anger of the crew: "What kind of high command have we that with such great force in operation we cannot fight it out? Have the British become gun-shy? How can wars be won this way?"

Commander Broome, as leader of the close escort, then took matters in his own hands. He sent his six destroyers to lend support to the departed cruiser force in the battle he assumed was about to take place with German warships. Broome left the two British submarines in the convoy area, lest the enemy ships show up there. He ordered the other escort ships to proceed independently to Archangel; a few of them, however, chose to accompany whatever merchant ships they could.

But most of the merchant ships were left to their own devices. Beginning early on July 5, the Luftwaffe and the U-boats pressed a relentless attack that lasted a week. On the first day, 12 of the merchant ships, as well as an oiler and a rescue ship, were hit and went down. On the 6th of July two more merchant ships were sunk; on the 7th, two more; on the 8th, one more; and on the 10th, two more.

The men who leaped from sinking vessels plunged into icy waters coated with flaming oil. If they managed to get into lifeboats, they were still 200 miles or more from land. If they reached shore, they might have hundreds of miles to go before finding a settlement.

Of the 35 merchant ships that had set out for Archangel, only 11 reached the Russian port. Of these, one small group of three ships owed its survival to an officer of one of the escort vessels that had chosen to stay the course. It was his bright idea to paint the ships white to blend with the background of ice, and to further camouflage their topsides with sheets. German search planes flew over them—and thanks to the white paint and a fortuitous fog, did not spot them. The last of the ships limped into Archangel—450 miles from the point where the convoy had dispersed—on July 24, three weeks after the crippling order to scatter. If the convoy had kept to its original schedule, it would have made the entire voyage in 12 days.

When all losses had been tallied, the toll was appalling: 153 men had been lost and 22 merchant ships had been sunk—and with them a cargo of 430 tanks, 210 aircraft and 99,316 tons of miscellaneous war goods. Of the 1,300 men who made it to Archangel—some in their original ships, others picked up by British escorts and Soviet rescue vessels—many were maimed by frostbite, incurred in the icy waters. Two dozen unlucky survivors, having rowed for 10 days in a lifeboat in what they thought was the direction of Russia, landed instead in German-occupied Norway, and ended up in a prison camp.

A final ironic twist came to light later on. At the time the Admiralty was sending out its frantic orders to PQ-17 to scatter, the *Tirpitz* was not advancing on the convoy at all, but had simply moved from one Norwegian port to another. German patrol planes had spotted and then lost track of the aircraft carrier *Victorious* of PQ-17's distant covering force, and Hitler had no intention of exposing his battleship to the risk of air attack.

The only thing to be said for the PQ-17 episode was that it taught a bitter and costly lesson, making clear the necessity of keeping a convoy under the constant vigilance of well-coordinated escort vessels. So long as the ships of PQ-17 had stayed together, only three had come to grief; the debacle occurred after the scattering. It was a lesson that was to be driven home again in the critical months ahead.

THE SEA WAR ON CANVAS

German war artist Adolf Boch painted this surfaced U-boat shelling an armed merchant cruiser with her 88mm gun, a quick-firing, general-purpose weapon.

CAPTURING THE ATLANTIC ACTION

Aboard the destroyer *Niblack* in the murky dawn of October 31, 1941, U.S. Navy artist Griffith Baily Coale saw a rising cloud of black smoke a mile ahead. Moments later there was a tremendous roar and a column of orange flame leaped into the night sky. The U.S. destroyer *Reuben James,* escorting a convoy bound for Britain, had just been torpedoed. Coale's ship rushed to the scene. As the *Niblack's* men pulled oil-soaked survivors from the freezing water, the artist could hear "cursing, praying and hoarse shouts for help." Coale could not forget the horror: his drawing at left of the blazing destroyer—the first American combat ship to be sunk in the Atlantic—has an immediacy and impact only the luckiest of photographers could have captured.

Scores of artists covered the sea war from both sides, and in many ways their art offers the best record of the fighting's most dramatic moments. A photographer was not always able to catch these events, but often a painter could watch the drama unfold and later put down on either a sketch pad or canvas the scenes that had been burned into his consciousness.

If the artist was commissioned in the Navy, he had additional duties afloat, usually serving as an officer of the watch. When fighting erupted, he rarely got much chance to draw; instead he manned a battle station like everyone else aboard. Only afterward did he go on duty as an artist to set down the conflict from his vivid recollection.

The popular American painter Tom Lea, working aboard the U.S. destroyer *Gleaves* in the fall of 1941 on assignment for LIFE, made it a practice to memorize what he saw on deck; then he went below to make sketches and later produced his finished paintings back home in Texas. "With the water slopping in," he recalled, "you couldn't do watercolor. You couldn't even sketch out there; it was like a bucking bronco."

The paintings by Lea and other seafaring artists enabled thousands at home in America and Europe to experience both the peaks of combat and the tense hours between peaks *(right)* in one of the War's most violent arenas.

Flames shoot up into the sky from the torpedoed U.S. destroyer Reuben James in Lieut. Commander Griffith Baily Coale's drawing of the sinking.

A red-scarved U-boat commander and some of his crew scan the seas for prey in a painting by German artist Rudolf Hausknecht.

"Tossing the Cans" by LIFE artist Tom Lea
captures the action aboard the American
destroyer Gleaves as members of her crew fire
depth charges. The mortar that fired
the canisters was known as a Y-gun; it was
operated by an explosive charge.

"A Kill in Biscay," painted by U.S. Navy Lieutenant Dwight Shepler, shows a Navy PB4Y depth-bombing a U-boat.

Gunners of the U.S. destroyer Champlin aim at unidentified planes over a convoy in this Dwight Shepler watercolor.

Covered by a comrade with a submachine gun, a rescue party from the U.S. Coast Guard cutter Campbell takes aboard survivors from a sinking U-boat. LIFE artist Lieut. Commander Anton Otto Fischer, who painted the dramatic scene, was on board the Campbell when she attacked the sub at point-blank range in the North Atlantic in 1943.

A sheet of fire runs along the side of the German heavy cruiser Prinz Eugen as she and the battleship Bismarck (left) unleash broadsides against the British

battle cruiser Hood, in a canvas by German artist Claus Bergen. In the May 1941 battle, the Hood was sunk by half a dozen salvos from the two warships.

The sighting of the Bismarck at sea by the
British Catalina Z209 on May 26, 1941, is the
subject of this dramatic canvas by English artist
Norman Wilkinson. On the following day,
the elusive German battleship was sunk in a
battle with ships of the Royal Navy.

British Swordfish torpedo bombers attack the German battleships Scharnhorst and Gneisenau (right foreground) on February 12, 1942, in this painting by Norman Wilkinson. All of the planes that took part in this mission were shot down by the German warships.

A cluster of bright flares illuminates the action in Englishman Charles

Pears's painting as the Scharnhorst (right background) comes under mortal fire during the Battle of North Cape off the coast of Norway, December 26, 1943.

Silhouetted in the glare of a searchlight, a ship torpedoed by a U-boat hovers for a moment at the perpendicular before sliding beneath the waves. The German

artist Julius Caesar Schmitz-Westerholt included one of the submariners in the foreground to personalize the drama.

7

On the afternoon of June 15, 1942, an American merchant seaman named Archie Gibbs found himself floundering in the waters of the Caribbean for the second time in 24 hours. The day before, somewhere north of Trinidad, a U-boat had torpedoed his ship, the *Scottsburg.* After a night in the sea, he had been picked up by the Matson Line's freighter *Kahuku*—only to land in the drink again when she too was sunk by a U-boat.

Now Gibbs faced a third peril. As he was struggling to stay afloat, the U-boat surfaced close by. In desperation, he tried to swim away but, as he later reported, "they swept the stern around, submerged a little, and came right up under me. A big German grabbed me by the neck and gave me the bum's rush up to the conning tower."

Gibbs feared the worst. Inside the sub, an officer thrust a gun under his nose and ordered him to take a whiff of the end of the barrel, suggesting the fate in store for him if he failed to tell the truth about the ships on which he had served. But under grilling, Gibbs managed to sound so plausible that when it was over his captors were pleased enough to treat him to a swig of brandy.

That was just one of the indulgences Gibbs enjoyed for the next four days. He shared the crew's hearty fare of stew, cabbage, bacon and bread; he was allowed to witness a rendezvous between the U-boat and her milch-cow supplier, in which she took on a new load of torpedoes. On the fifth day, off Curaçao, Gibbs's unexpected odyssey ended. Sighting a Venezuelan motor vessel, his captors put him aboard a raft and waved him off to freedom.

The treatment accorded Gibbs jibed with the experience of other survivors of Caribbean sinkings. Two sailors off the tanker *M. F. Elliott* were taken aboard the attacking U-boat, scrubbed clean of the oil that encrusted them, given dry clothing and some warming rum, then put out on a raft at a point where a rescue plane was circling overhead. The captain of the torpedoed *Esso Houston*, settling into a lifeboat after the tanker went down, was startled to find himself face to face with the commander of the offending U-boat— come alongside to make sure the lifeboat was adequately stocked with food, water, medicine and compass.

The Germans had reason to be magnanimous. The Caribbean was a submariner's dream of a tour of duty. It had none of the Arctic rigors of the Murmansk route, none of

THE FINAL ROUND

the storms of the North Atlantic. The island-studded Caribbean offered many an isolated cove where a U-boat could put in unseen and debark its crew for hours of sunning on coral sands and bathing in crystal waters. On uninhabited islands the men hunted game; elsewhere they had little trouble persuading natives to provide them with fresh vegetables and, occasionally, female company.

But the Caribbean had other advantages as well. Sinking ships there was proving wonderfully easy. Vessels outbound from ports in Cuba, Puerto Rico, Central America, Panama and Venezuela traveled not in convoys but independently, as vulnerable to hostile action as the old sailing ships had been to Caribbean buccaneers.

Nor were ships moving in and out of American ports on the Gulf of Mexico immune. By ranging slightly farther afield, the U-boats were able to play hob with shipping off Galveston, New Orleans, Mobile, Tampa.

Admiral Dönitz was now headquartered in Paris; he had moved from Lorient in March in the wake of a devastating British air-and-sea raid on nearby Saint-Nazaire. But any embarrassment caused by this enforced transfer was forgotten in the good news from across the Atlantic. Hanging in the new offices of the German submarine command on the Avenue Maréchal in Paris was a wall map of the Caribbean and the Gulf. It bristled with gold-headed pins, each denoting a ship sent to the bottom, a cargo denied to the Allies: tin from Venezuela and bauxite from Dutch Guiana, essential to building up America's arsenal; such cherished staples of the American diet as Cuban sugar and Colombian coffee. There was also another kind of cargo of more immediate consequence. As ordered, the U-boats were making tankers their chief target; as a result, much of the lost tonnage was high-octane aviation gasoline from the Dutch refineries at Aruba, intended to fuel Britain's RAF bombers in their continuing assault against German-held Europe.

Surveying the proliferating pins on his wall, Dönitz exuded satisfaction. To him they symbolized more than a series of kills; they told him his strategy was working.

That strategy was based on two convictions. Dönitz felt certain that the key to victory in the Battle of the Atlantic lay in the amount of enemy tonnage he could destroy; so long as his U-boats kept sinking large quantities of Allied shipping, steadily adding to his box score, any one area of the Atlantic served the purpose as well as another. At the same time Dönitz believed in avoiding undue risks—in minimizing his losses while maximizing the enemy's.

These twin convictions meant that as soon as the enemy strengthened its convoy defenses in one part of the ocean, Dönitz would order his submarines to another area, where they could operate at less hazard to themselves while continuing to pile up enemy kills. And they could travel far and wide. The bigger U-boats, 1,100-tonners, had a cruising range of about 13,000 miles. The medium-sized 750-tonners had a range of about 8,500 miles, and could be refueled by the milch cows at convenient points en route.

At the beginning of the War, Dönitz had attacked British ships in the Western Approaches off the southwest coast of Britain. Early in 1942, as Britain improved its convoy system, he had dispatched his submarines to patrol off Iceland, Greenland and Canada. The Canadians' growing expertise at convoy protection and America's entry into the War had led him to move the U-boats south to the East Coast of the United States. There Dönitz had reaped a rich harvest of Allied shipping until the Americans set up an effective interlocking convoy system to provide escort protection along their entire Eastern Seaboard. Now his U-boats had moved to the Caribbean and the Gulf of Mexico—where most ships still traveled without convoy protection.

Dönitz racked up a heavy score of Allied shipping in the Caribbean and the Gulf: some 750,000 tons in just three months. But in pursuing easy pickings, Dönitz was giving the Allies a vital respite where they needed it most. His concentration on the Caribbean and the Gulf was forcing him to neglect the battle's most important arena: the northern routes by which Britain was supplied with food, arms and other wartime necessities. One of Britain's most seasoned convoy commanders, Captain Donald Macintyre, was to look back on the summer of 1942 in the North Atlantic as "amazingly quiet," a time when the convoys in his charge "ploughed peacefully to and fro across the Atlantic with never a sight of a U-boat."

But as far as Dönitz was concerned, the strategy was paying off handsomely in terms of enemy tonnage sunk. The toll in the months ahead promised to be even higher. With new U-boats coming down the ways at the rate of 30 a month, Germany's total submarine fleet now numbered

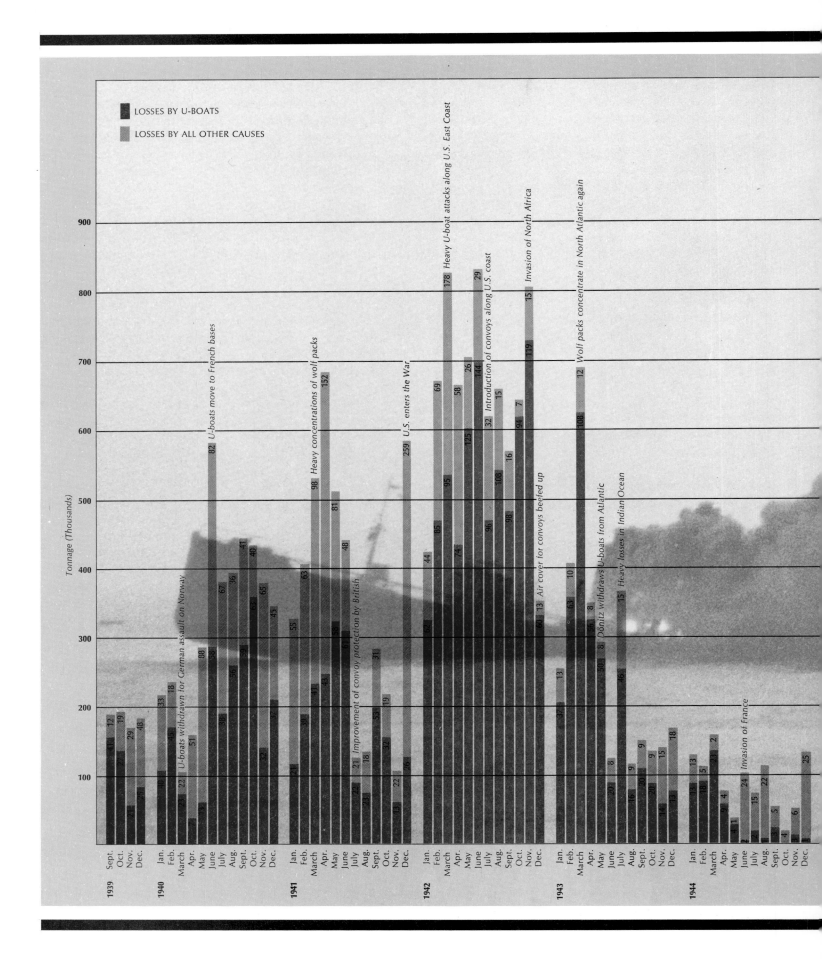

LOSSES BY U-BOATS

LOSSES BY ALL OTHER CAUSES

Tonnage (Thousands)

900

800

700

600

500

400

300

200

100

U-boats move to French bases 82

Heavy concentrations of wolf packs 152

U.S. enters the War 259

Heavy U-boat attacks along U.S. East Coast 178

Introduction of convoys along U.S. coast 29

Invasion of North Africa 15

Wolf packs concentrate in North Atlantic again 12

U-boats withdrawn for German assault on Norway

Improvement of convoy protection by British

Air cover for convoys beefed up

Dönitz withdraws U-boats from Atlantic

Heavy losses in Indian Ocean

Invasion of France

1939 — Sept. Oct. Nov. Dec.

1940 — Jan. Feb. March Apr. May June July Aug. Sept. Oct. Nov. Dec.

1941 — Jan. Feb. March Apr. May June July Aug. Sept. Oct. Nov. Dec.

1942 — Jan. Feb. March Apr. May June July Aug. Sept. Oct. Nov. Dec.

1943 — Jan. Feb. March Apr. May June July Aug. Sept. Oct. Nov. Dec.

1944 — Jan. Feb. March Apr. May June July Aug. Sept. Oct. Nov. Dec.

THE UPS AND DOWNS OF SHIPPING LOSSES

The skyscraper-like graph shown at left—compiled from figures released by the British Admiralty after the War—dramatizes the ebb and flow of the Battle of the Atlantic as first one side and then the other gained the upper hand. Although the diagram includes Allied ships sunk all over the world throughout the War, only 10 per cent were sunk outside the Atlantic.

Shipping losses are represented on the chart in thousands of tons (figures on left), while the numbers of ships sunk in each month appear in the vertical bars. U-boat sinkings (dark red) were, of course, the biggest source of ship casualties, accounting for more than two thirds of the toll. Other causes (light red) included mines, surface raiders and aircraft.

During the early months of the battle, when only a few U-boats were operating in the Atlantic and convoy protection had not been extended over most of the shipping routes, the sinkings were confined mostly to individual vessels or stragglers. Shipping losses soared in the summer of 1940, however, when the fall of France enabled the German submarines to move down from the north and swarm out of French bases in what became known as the Happy Time—a period when they sank 217 ships totaling more than one million tons. To counter this onslaught, Britain integrated air cover with surface escorts and extended the range of convoy protection.

The U.S. entry into the War brought with it a U-boat blitz in American waters at the beginning of 1942 and the Battle of the Atlantic's heaviest shipping losses. Before coastal convoys could be established, 137 ships of 828,000 tons were sunk along the East Coast and in the Bermuda area.

But by the spring of 1943 the tide was shifting as antisubmarine tactics improved. For the next two years the Germans fought a battle of diminishing returns in the Atlantic, losing one and a half U-boats for every merchant ship that they sent to the bottom. When it was finally over, the war at sea in all areas had claimed more than 4,600 merchant ships totaling more than 21 million tons—plus 785 U-boats.

300. By October, nearly 200 of them—more than twice as many as before—would be in operation all at once, ready to go where Dönitz ordered them.

In July, when the United States extended its convoy system all the way to Trinidad, Dönitz realized that the pickings would no longer be easy in the Caribbean area. In the meantime, however, his U-boats had already been ranging farther south. They had sunk seven Brazilian ships, and he decided now to concentrate his main effort in the Brazil area, where there was a lengthy and largely unguarded coastline that promised a new bonanza in sunken tonnage. The auguries looked particularly good when, shortly after the U-boats' arrival, one of them sank five Brazilian freighters off the state of Bahia in little more than 24 hours.

It was a remarkable feat—and a major diplomatic blunder. The earlier sinkings of Brazilian ships had taken place as far as 1,200 miles out to sea, and over a period of weeks. But the newest sinkings, in such quick succession and close to shore, stirred profound shock. When the news reached Rio de Janeiro, riots erupted. The windows of German-owned shops were smashed, Nazi flags trampled and burned. A week later, Brazil declared war on Germany.

The benefit to the Allies was huge. Unofficially, Brazil had long favored the Allied cause, even extending its Navy's help in patrolling South American waters. But its formal entry into the War meant that the Allies could now operate from Brazilian bases, using them as handy jump-off points to thwart enemy forays anywhere in the South Atlantic, including the west coast of Africa. Many an Allied ship, traveling to and from the Far East by way of the Cape of Good Hope, had turned into a tonnage statistic for Dönitz.

The Allies thus had less to worry about on their southern flank when, early in November, they launched Operation Torch, the North African invasion that signaled their first massive counterattack in the European-African theater of operations. Dönitz had a number of U-boats in the area from the Bay of Biscay to the Cape Verde Islands; he ordered them to speed toward the coast of North Africa. The submarines arrived too late to halt the initial landings, but they did damage three American transports off the tiny port of Fedala, just north of Casablanca. They hovered near debarkation ports and outside the Straits of Gibraltar. Although a British supply ship and a destroyer were hit, Allied convoy protection proved so strong Dönitz had to move his U-boats west into waters not so heavily patrolled.

The pickings were getting slimmer for Dönitz everywhere he turned. By now he had concluded that the best opportunity for his U-boats lay in a return in force to the North Atlantic, reviving the wolf-pack technique. In going back there Dönitz knew he risked higher U-boat losses from the better organized escorts now accompanying the Allied convoys, but his options were steadily growing more limited.

The area that Dönitz selected for the revival of the wolf-pack attacks was a stretch of water several hundred miles wide, extending from a point south of Greenland to roughly midway across the ocean, a part of the Atlantic that was out of range of land-based aircraft—whether from Greenland, Iceland, the United Kingdom or North America. Carrier-based planes had not joined the battle at this point.

Once in this so-called Greenland air gap—more ruefully known to veteran sailors as "the black pit"—the U-boats could operate with relative impunity. Dönitz had them form picket lines at both ends of the gap, ready to pounce on ships entering it either from the west or the east. By now, he could concentrate more U-boats than ever for the largest wolf-pack attack of the War. The results were staggering. By November's end, the admiral could add 637,000 tons—a new monthly high—to his score of Allied shipping destroyed. Then over the next two months the totals dropped sharply as U-boats and convoys alike fought an enemy too powerful to contain: winter weather even worse than that of the year before, with gales of extraordinary ferocity.

In January, Captain John Waters Jr. of the United States Coast Guard was on the cutter *Ingham*, escorting a convoy westbound out of Iceland, when the ships met what he later called "a killer hurricane the likes of which even the saltiest seaman had seldom encountered before." Waters reported waves 60 feet high. "The tops of the towering seas were torn off by the howling winds, carrying spray hundreds of feet into the air and reducing visibility to near zero."

While the storms raged on, a meeting that was to prove crucial to the Battle of the Atlantic took place on the palm-fringed coast of North Africa. The skies were cloudless and the breezes balmy, but the conferees—Roosevelt, Churchill and their military chiefs—were in less than a holiday mood.

The conference was shrouded in great secrecy: barbed wire and heavily armed guards surrounded the hotel outside Casablanca where the Allied leaders reviewed the war, theater by theater, and threshed out their future course.

By the end of the 10-day meeting, priorities had been set—and top priority was waging war on the U-boats. More than material resources were to be involved; American, British and Canadian antisubmarine commands were henceforth to synchronize their efforts more effectively.

News of the Casablanca Conference was announced only after FDR and Churchill were safely home. The communiqué said little more than that "a more intense prosecution of the war by sea, land and air" was in prospect; it concluded with high resolve: "The President and Prime Minister and their combined staffs, having completed their plans for the offensive campaigns of 1943, have now separated in order to put them into active and concerted execution."

Admiral Dönitz was not at all dismayed by the implications of the enemy communiqué. Five days after the news broke, the Führer appointed him commander in chief of the entire German Navy, replacing Grand Admiral Raeder, who had held the post for 15 years. Raeder's downfall came after the dismal performance of two of his proudest ships, the pocket battleship *Lützow* and the heavy cruiser *Hipper*, in an attack on an Allied convoy off Norway on the last day of December 1942. For four hours they had been held off by five escorting British destroyers; they damaged only one merchantman. Two British cruisers eventually showed up and drove them off. Hitler, infuriated, had tongue-lashed Raeder for 90 minutes, then named him Inspector-General of the Navy—a trivial post created for the occasion.

Dönitz, a keen student of Nazi palace politics, was sure he could steer the hazardous shoals between Hitler's flimsy notions of naval warfare and his own hardheaded views. Moreover, he now had the authority to allot German naval resources without going through admirals who outranked him. In his new status, and with Hitler's backing, he could lavish whatever he thought was needed—added U-boats, personnel, equipment—on his beloved submarine service.

With some improvement in the weather, the month of March brought his greatest triumph. In the first 10 days alone, the U-boats sank 41 ships; in the second 10 days they bagged 54—some 500,000 tons in all. By month's end, Al-

In their war against U-boats, the Allies developed an ungainly-looking, multiple-barreled weapon called the Hedgehog (top) that fired a barrage of 24 small bombs in an oval pattern over a wide area (bottom picture). Before the development of this weapon, submarine-killers employing depth charges had to pass directly over a submerged U-boat. Hedgehogs could be fired up to 250 yards ahead of the ship. Because their bombs were equipped with contact fuses, the missiles exploded *only* when a hit was scored—and were almost always fatal.

lied losses stood at 567,000 tons. Though somewhat less than the all-time high of the previous November, the sinkings were more significant: two thirds were ships traveling not alone but in convoys. In one convoy, 13 of 51 ships went down with no loss to the attackers; in another, 21 of 90 ships went down, and only one of 40 U-boats was sunk.

At the Admiralty in London, despair engulfed the men who labored to improve the convoy system. Later they were to record their belief that the Germans never came closer to "disrupting communications between the New World and the Old" than in the first 20 days of March 1943.

Britain's official naval historian, Captain Stephen W. Roskill, summed up the dilemma succinctly. In three and a half years of war, he wrote, the convoy system had become the "lynch pin of our maritime strategy. Where could the Admiralty turn if the convoy system had lost its effectiveness? They did not know; but they must have felt, though no one admitted it, that defeat then stared them in the face."

Yet in just two months an astonishing turnaround occurred. In April, the toll exacted by the U-boats dropped to 277,000 tons—less than half that of March. In May, it dropped to 212,000 tons. Even more gratifying to the Allies was the rise in U-boat losses: 15 sunk in April, 41 in May.

The sudden reversal of Allied fortunes seemed a near miracle; it was, in fact, the culmination of many long months of slogging effort by the people with every sort of skill in every corner of the Allied camp. Physicists painstakingly improved detection devices and technicians trained in their use. Statisticians assessed the effects of weapons in combat. Military planners reconciled differences on strategy and corrected errors in tactics.

The entire effort was akin to assembling a gigantic and uniquely challenging jigsaw puzzle. And in the late spring of 1943 the pieces finally fell into place.

By then, the tonnage produced per month in Allied shipyards far surpassed the tonnage lost to U-boats. The Americans alone were performing prodigies of production: in the single month of April, they built more than one million tons of merchant shipping—quadruple the nation's output for all of 1939. In addition to this feat the United States was increasing its construction of naval vessels designed for better defense of the convoys and for a more slashing offensive against the U-boats: compact new escort carriers capable of accommodating up to 30 planes, and sleek destroyer escorts with speeds from 17 to 24 knots.

The increasing numbers of available escort vessels, along with the higher speed of the new merchant ships, made it possible for most vital cargoes to sail in fast convoys with a new and more effective antisubmarine formation: the so-called "bent-line screen." Instead of circling the convoy on all sides, the escorts now traveled ahead of the merchant ships, with some directly in front and at least one on each bow. The new formation protected the convoy from the most probable area of attack—U-boats lying in wait up ahead—while the speed of the convoy itself diminished the possibility of effective submarine attack from the rear.

In the skies, Allied capabilities were steadily expanding. Month by month, the Greenland air gap was being narrowed, and U-boats found themselves under bombing attack in areas they had assumed no shore-based plane could reach. Both east and west of the gap—in Britain, Greenland, Iceland and Newfoundland—airfield runways were crowded with the best planes aeronautic engineering could provide: such long-range aircraft as the Flying Fortress and the Catalina, with an operational radius of 400 to 600 miles from base, and the very long-range Liberator, which could travel as far as 1,000 miles from base, then patrol for four hours before having to head back.

These aircraft, reaching ever deeper into the Greenland air gap, turned what had been a virtual playground for the German subs into a death trap. More than one U-boat commander, suddenly faced with a savage assault from on high, may have given a fleeting thought to a remark made by Dönitz early in the War and widely circulated among his men. "An aircraft can no more kill a U-boat," he had said, "than a crow can kill a mole."

By now Dönitz had exchanged this conviction for another. He was sure the precision with which the planes homed in on the U-boats could mean only that there was treason in his own ranks. But an investigation turned up nothing. What was betraying the location of the U-boats was a product of British ingenuity: a new variety of radar operating on microwave frequencies. Though the earlier, longer-wave versions had served the Allies brilliantly, this one was more accurate and more powerful. It could be housed so compactly and required so small an antenna that it was easily installed on a boat or fitted into a plane.

Dönitz, of course, was aware of the existence of radar—his own countrymen were making large strides with it—but this new so-called centimetric radar was still a closely guarded Allied secret.

British specialists had long pondered the problem of developing a radar beam so sharp that the echoes it evoked from a potential target would not be hampered by the interference that the waves of the sea posed as the beam struck them. To obtain a sharp beam required either the use of a very large antenna—cumbersome for ships and even more so for planes—or the use of extremely short wavelengths, measured in centimeters rather than in the meters of long-wave radar. The shorter the wavelength, the narrower the beam that was produced, cutting down on interference and pinpointing the target not only with greater accuracy but also with greater clarity.

What was needed was a transmitter that could give out pulses of very high power at wavelengths of a few centimeters. In late 1939 two British physicists at Birmingham University, Dr. John Randall and Harry Boot, invented such a device, called the resonant cavity magnetron. One man who saw it described it as a "finely turned squat cylinder of brass about the size of a flat tin of pipe tobacco."

The size proved to have a far-reaching side effect. A prototype of the cavity magnetron was small enough to fit into a black box, containing blueprints and other secret data, that was brought to the United States in August 1940 by a delegation of top-ranking British scientists headed by Sir Henry Tizard. At that time Britain was fighting the Germans by itself, and expecting them to invade momentarily. The Tizard mission, which proposed to give the Americans Britain's scientific secrets in exchange for American scientific help in various crucial research ventures, was notably successful after the cavity magnetron was demonstrated. "The most valuable cargo ever brought to our shores," one American pronounced it. The era of microwave radar was launched, and by mid-1943 enough Allied ships and planes were equipped with the radar sets to create wholesale havoc among the U-boats.

The Germans had a protective radar-detection device, but it worked only with long-wave radar. Called Metox, it consisted of an aerial in the shape of a cross, made of wood and strung with wires, installed on the U-boat's conning tower; a cable running down the hatch connected it to controls inside the sub. Impulses picked up by the wires indicated that the U-boat was caught in the enemy's radar beam, providing enough advance warning to allow the captain to order a crash dive.

But Metox had serious drawbacks, even aside from its inability to detect short-wave signals. It had to be hastily dismantled and thrown down the hatch before the U-boat submerged, and had to be reassembled before it could be used again. Moreover, its own signals were inconsistent, varying from a buzz to a nerve-racking whistle. Often a

Britain's roughhewn Admiral Sir Max Horton (right, center), chief of Western Approaches after November 1942, and austere, authoritarian Admiral Ernest J. King (above), commander in chief of the U.S. Navy, masterminded victory in the Atlantic. Although they consulted each other constantly, they never met.

TAKING A PRIZE TROPHY IN TOW

Under cover of a U.S. Navy torpedo bomber, a boarding party takes over the deserted German sub U-505. In the background, a U.S. destroyer stands watch.

Beneath a tranquil sea on June 4, 1944, lunch was being served to the crew of the *U-505*, headed homeward after patrolling Africa's Gold Coast. Suddenly the boat was buffeted by depth charges from the U.S.S. *Chatelain*, part of a six-ship American task force commanded by Captain Daniel V. Gallery. The violent explosions sent food, crockery and sailors flying to the deck. Some of the men thought the sub was sinking and rushed for the conning tower escape hatch. First Lieutenant Harald Lange, the *U-505's* skipper, immediately brought the 740-ton boat to the surface,

where she was promptly peppered with fire from the *Chatelain*, two other U.S. destroyers and two Grumman Wildcats from Gallery's flagship, the carrier *Guadalcanal*.

Terrified, the U-boat's crew scrambled through the hatch, frantically waved their hands and jumped overboard. The submarine's rudder had been jammed and as the U-boat circled aimlessly, a boarding party from the U.S. destroyer *Pillsbury* moved in to seize the coveted prize. A whaleboat pulled alongside, and Lieutenant (jg.) Albert L. David leaped on board. Followed by two petty officers, he boldly plunged

through the conning tower hatch, risking death from demolition charges or from enemy crew members still below (he later received the Congressional Medal of Honor for his swift, decisive action).

The U-boat was now completely deserted but rapidly filling with water. David and his companions immediately gathered up charts, code books and other important papers, closed the submarine's valves and secured her engines.

Pumps were rigged to help keep the sub afloat, and a heavy wire hawser from the *Guadalcanal* was fastened to the U-boat.

The U-505's capture was planned by Captain Daniel Gallery (left) and executed by a daring team led by Lieutenant (jg.) Albert David (right). A receipt (below) records the sub's delivery to the U.S. Navy in Bermuda.

Bermuda, B.W.I.,
June 19, 1944.

Received from Commander E. Trosino, U.S.N.R. (representing Captain D. V. Gallery, U.S.N.) the German submarine U-505 which was captured at sea by Task Group 22.3.

Signed _W. N. Christensen_
Rank _Comdr U.S.N._
Representing _Commodore_

As 40 surviving submariners watched grimly from the *Chatelain's* decks, the carrier took the German vessel in tow, a large U.S. flag flying from her conning tower.

Because the closest port was at Dakar, which teemed with German sympathizers, Gallery headed for Bermuda, 1,700 miles away. After four days, an American tug took over the chore of towing the U-boat, and on June 19, the little tug entered Port Royal Bay, Bermuda, with the *U-505* trailing in her wake—the first enemy vessel captured on the high seas by an American force since the War of 1812.

In the conning tower of the U-505, Captain Gallery enjoys his booty after the U-boat's capture. The captain boarded the sub to check for a booby trap falsely reported to be attached to the door of a torpedo room.

U-boat commander had the apparatus switched off simply "in order to remain sane," as one of them put it.

The Germans got their first intimation of the enemy's powerful new centimetric radar in February 1943. In a routine examination of the wreckage of an RAF bomber shot down near Rotterdam, German Air Force inspectors found a bloodstained box with "Experimental 6" penciled on the side. It went to a Luftwaffe laboratory in Berlin for scrutiny; though the apparatus was badly damaged, enough evidence remained to make the experts suspect the British had developed a type of radar deemed impossible by the Germans.

Under orders from Luftwaffe chief Hermann Göring, intensive research began. In March the RAF scored a direct hit on the laboratory; engineers frantically scrambled through the still-smoking ruins and retrieved the apparatus. When a German model at last was completed, it was tested at the top of a radio tower with results that flabbergasted the testers. In spite of low visibility, objects 20 miles distant showed up on the radar screen in extraordinary detail. Among those present at the test was a delegation from the German Navy; as a historian later described it, they "took one look at the radar set and knew why there had been such dreadful U-boat losses during the past months."

Göring immediately ordered Germany's electronics industry to set to work building a German version of centimetric radar; he assigned an even higher priority to developing a receiver that could detect the British version, and had 10,000 technicians released from the armed forces to help. But by the time the effort bore fruit, the tide in the Battle of the Atlantic had swung overwhelmingly in the Allies' favor.

Ultimately, Allied triumph in the Atlantic had to depend on the men who determined how all the ships, planes and technology could best be organized and employed. The built-in complexities of the task were compounded by the widely divergent ways in which the British and the Americans traditionally ran their navies. The differences ranged from tactics and command setups to gunnery, signaling and other communications methods. In the Royal Navy there were those who thought American procedures "immature." The Americans deemed British procedures "obsolete."

Lack of coordination had caused a number of convoy disasters in 1942, and had so deeply concerned Roosevelt and Churchill that at Casablanca in January 1943 they had scheduled a full-dress conference of their military chiefs on the subject. The conferees met in Washington in March and found a solution that was both neat and diplomatic. Aware of the explosive issues of national pride and sovereignty, they rejected proposals for a unified Allied antisubmarine command and instead set up three coequal commands: American, British and Canadian, each one running its own show—and using its own procedures.

The formula was the brain child of Admiral Ernest J. King, commander in chief of the United States Navy. It divided control of the North Atlantic convoys between the British and the Canadians, each from their own shores to a mid-ocean point called the "chop line," which was fixed at longitude 47° W. The only part of the North Atlantic route assigned to the Americans was the short run between New York and Halifax. The Americans were to control the convoys that crossed the Central Atlantic from the Eastern Seaboard and the Caribbean to Gibraltar and North Africa; they were also to have charge of tanker convoys going from the Dutch West Indies direct to Britain—to ease the strain imposed on British and Canadian escort vessels by their increased burdens in the North Atlantic. Long-range aircraft, whether British, Canadian or American, were to work anywhere they were needed; their only limit was to be their own operational radius.

By clearly delineating spheres of responsibility, Admiral King's solution markedly improved relations within the Allied camp. Sources of friction were eliminated. Each Ally was now at liberty to deal with matters within its command in its own way.

King himself, soon after the Washington conference, set up a curious entity he named the Tenth Fleet. It was a fleet that never went to sea: it had no ships, only shore-based sailors and comparatively few officers, among whom was King as commander.

The Tenth Fleet's purpose was to transform the American antisubmarine effort into a paragon of efficiency. Up to now it had been a haphazard affair; operating units were more or less autonomous, with their own tactical planners and intelligence staffs. Henceforth the Tenth Fleet was to direct every aspect of antisubmarine activity, deciding convoy routes, allocating escort groups, serving as a clearing-

Her decks jammed with American soldiers, the passenger liner Queen Mary sets sail alone from America to Europe. The 81,235-ton ship could maintain a steady speed of 28½ knots, so fast that submarines could not catch up with her or keep her in their sights. Put into service as a troop transport in August 1942, she traveled without escort carrying as many as 15,000 troops, the equivalent of a whole division.

house for U-boat information, and correlating antisubmarine research and matériel development.

The happiest additions to the Tenth Fleet were some 30 civilians, all members of a hush-hush unit known both as Group M and, more formally, as the Asworgs (for Antisubmarine Warfare Operations Research Group). Drawn from among the country's finest mathematicians, physicists, chemists and biologists, the Asworgs devoted themselves to such intricate problems as the best angle at which a plane should swoop in on a U-boat, and which of 7,000 patterns of depth charges were the most effective.

Before the Tenth Fleet came into being, these dedicated researchers had felt the frustration of many wanderers in a bureaucratic maze. As one Navy archivist noted: "They had no central authority to whom suggestions could be reported and who could take action on the suggestions if action was deemed advisable." Under the Tenth Fleet, the Asworgs came into their own as full-fledged participants in the defeat of the U-boats.

In Britain, Admiral King's counterpart was Admiral Sir Max Horton, who also had some very strong ideas about how the Battle of the Atlantic could be finally won. Horton—dubbed by Dönitz "my own personal adversary-in-chief"—had replaced Sir Percy Noble as Commander-in-Chief, Western Approaches, in November 1942. He was a fearsome man to work for. One of his officers was later to write: "He had more personal charm than any man I have ever met, but he could be unbelievably cruel to those who fell by the wayside. There is a picture by Goya of a 'Grand Inquisitor' which suggests much the same characteristics."

Horton did not suffer fools, or bores, gladly. Once he halted a weather expert's discourse on "cold fronts" and "precipitation" by snapping: "D'you ever look out of the window?" At night, clad only in pajamas, he would roar into the Plotting Room at his headquarters, Derby House, and fire questions at the people tracking the course of a battle. "Why the hell not?" was one of his favorite queries.

An ace submarine commander in the First World War, Horton staunchly believed offensive measures against the U-boats must go hand-in-hand with defensive measures.

Up to a point the offensive measures that he advocated harked back to the early days of the War and the discredited tactics of search and destroy. But in critical respects Horton's methods differed markedly from those of 1940, when British warships had been sent off to rove wide expanses of ocean in haphazard and generally fruitless search of the enemy. For one thing, that effort had been undertaken at a time when Britain's naval resources were far more limited, and it had deprived the transatlantic convoys of the escort protection that they vitally needed. Now, however, Horton had a sufficient number of warships at his disposal to provide adequate convoy escorts.

Furthermore, Horton's so-called support groups, though separate and distinct from the escort groups, worked in concert with them. Ideally, the support groups included an escort carrier; more often, they were made up of destroyers, sloops or destroyer escorts. Their assignment was twofold: to hunt the attacking U-boats "to the death," and to reinforce an escort group whenever its convoy was threatened.

The new groups were instantly effective, and the Americans soon adopted the idea, calling their own units "hunter-killer groups." In accord with their flashier title, these units tended to operate more freely, roaming any areas where they suspected their quarries could be found. But in any event, the two Allies agreed so completely on the value of such units that at the Washington conference setting up separate commands they worked out a special arrangement. Though remaining under the strategic control of their own commands, the support groups were employed wherever they were most needed. Moreover, an American group, composed of the pioneer escort carrier U.S.S. *Bogue* and four destroyers, was detailed to operate under British direction in the North Atlantic.

The merit of Horton's concept was strikingly borne out in May 1943, in what was to be the climactic battle in the Atlantic, centering around a westbound convoy, ONS-5.

By the time it reached its various North American destinations Convoy ONS-5 had earned the unhappy distinction of being attacked by more U-boats—some 50 or 60—than any other in the War. Half of a 20-day crossing was spent in running fights with the enemy subs. In one day alone ONS-5 underwent 25 attacks.

The convoy seemed jinxed even before the first U-boat struck. Though the voyage began in late April, the weather was almost as foul as it had been in the dead of winter.

Adding to this difficulty was the fact that the 43 merchantmen in the convoy were lightly ballasted; they had deposited their cargoes in Britain, and were returning to Canadian and American ports to pick up new loads. In the rough seas, they found it next to impossible to keep even their slow speed or, more important, to stay on course. The British convoy escort—two destroyers, a frigate, four corvettes and two armed rescue trawlers—had to expand precious quantities of fuel rounding up stragglers.

Convoy ONS-5 was off Iceland and heading south toward Newfoundland when a U-boat slipped through the escort screen and sank the first victim: an American freighter, the *McKeesport*. At least seven other U-boats were driven off in hit-and-run sorties by the convoy escort under the direction of Commander Peter Gretton, who was a veteran of the transatlantic run.

Charting the progress of ONS-5 at his headquarters in Liverpool, Admiral Horton correctly surmised that further wolf-pack attacks awaited it. There were, in fact, at least three and possibly four such U-boat packs within range. A British support group of five destroyers happened to be at St. John's, in Newfoundland; Horton ordered it to go to the convoy's aid. It arrived none too soon; the fuel supply of Gretton's own ship, the destroyer *Duncan,* was running so low she would fast be a helpless target. Next day Gretton made a heart-wrenching decision: the *Duncan* left the convoy and made for St. John's. By the time she got there only 4 per cent of her fuel remained.

For the rest of the convoy, worse was to follow. Three of the support group's destroyers also had to leave the convoy because of dwindling fuel. Much of it had been expended on aggressive forays against the U-boats, and refueling in the rough seas was out of the question. Horton then ordered a second support group to the scene. But while it was on the way, ONS-5 suffered an unprecedented onslaught.

On the night of May 4, as the freighters were silhouetted against the northern lights, some 30 U-boats—working in twos and threes—poured torpedoes into the main body of the convoy and sank seven ships. Next morning they picked off four stragglers. Only one U-boat went down, victim of a relatively new weapon called the Hedgehog, installed on the corvette *Pink*. The Hedgehog was capable of launching 24 projectiles at a time, hurled from a multiple mortar on a ship's bow. Seven Hedgehog salvos disposed of the *U-192*.

As night fell on May 5, an unusually dense fog settled on the ocean. The U-boats, lacking radar, groped blindly; the convoy escort, equipped with centimetric radar, now had the advantage; it was able to fend off 25 attacks and sink two U-boats without the loss of a single ship.

Morale rose even higher the next day when the second support group arrived. One of its ships, the sloop *Pelican,* promptly dispatched the *U-438.* The corvette *Vidette* sank the *U-125.* A third U-boat barely escaped, its conning tower riddled by gunfire.

That day, ever alert to changing odds, Dönitz ordered all U-boats to break off and move east; if they lingered, they now faced attack by Allied aircraft from Newfoundland.

The ordeal of ONS-5 was over. It had lost almost a third of its ships. But Dönitz knew that in an earlier time so large a concentration of his U-boats would almost certainly have wiped out the entire convoy. The teamwork of the Allies' escort and support groups, together with their new technological devices, was making the difference.

Dönitz had further confirmation of this point in encounters between U-boats and convoys over the next few weeks. More than his declining tonnage score, what worried him was the increasing loss of U-boats. The total of 41 U-boat sinkings for May would be his greatest monthly loss in the battle to date, and in one of the wrecks littering the seabed would be the body of the Admiral's son.

The price was more than Dönitz cared to pay. He did not wait for the month-end tally. On the 24th, he withdrew all remaining U-boats from the North Atlantic, assuring Hitler that he intended to resume attacks there "at the time of the new moon." In his memoirs, years later, he was to be more candid. It was in the month of May 1943, he wrote, that he knew he had lost the Battle of the Atlantic.

The Allies could confirm the date on their own. In June of 1943, they began intensive preparations for Operation *Overlord*—the invasion of Normandy that was to be the first giant step in retaking Europe. Masses of men and matériel had to be sent across the North Atlantic, and that would be possible only if it was kept free of U-boats. In the year before *Overlord* was launched, German submarines sank only 92 ships of the thousands that were on the way to help ensure Germany's ultimate defeat.

AN OUTPOURING OF SHIPS

Rows of Liberty ships, nicknamed "Ugly Ducklings," await final outfitting in California before sailing through the Panama Canal for duty in the Atlantic.

DOWN THE WAYS IN 80 HOURS

One reason why the Allies were able to win the Battle of the Atlantic was that the United States could build ships faster than Germany could sink them. In 1939-1940 only 102 seagoing ships were constructed in the U.S. But in September 1941, the nation launched a crash program, mustering all of its industrial skills to produce a doughty vessel called the Liberty ship. By the end of 1942, 646 freighters had been completed, 597 of them Liberties, and launchings outnumbered sinkings in the Atlantic for the first time. By 1943, 140 Liberty ships were being launched each month.

At yards all over the country, 1.5 million workers learned to rivet and weld prefabricated components. The 441-foot ship they built—working without letup and at the surprisingly low cost of two million dollars per hull—was a homely adaptation of a British tramp steamer. She could travel 17,000 miles at 11 knots, using old-fashioned steam engines. She was not pretty or fast, but her straight lines and flat planes made her simple and quick to build, and she could carry 10,800 tons of badly needed cargo.

The genius behind this miracle of manufacture was bald and portly Henry J. Kaiser, a 60-year-old California contractor, who had completed the mammoth Boulder, Bonneville and Grand Coulee dams ahead of schedule. The secret to rapid ship construction, Kaiser realized, was to build as much as possible on dry land. Components were assembled all over the country. Freight cars carried them to shipyards, where they were stacked in a "filing system" along the ways where hulls were being built. When a hull was ready, cranes lifted bulkheads, fuel tanks, decks and superstructures into place. Once the hulls were launched, tugs towed them to finishing areas, where engines were installed and all equipment a ship would need at sea was put aboard.

At the peak of the wartime effort, workers constructed one ship in 80 hours and 30 minutes. So fast were the shipbuilders that a joke was told of a woman who stepped up with a champagne bottle, ready to christen a new ship. The keel had not even been laid. "What shall I do now?" she asked Kaiser. "Just start swinging," he said.

Shipbuilding wizard Henry J. Kaiser assembles a prefab model Liberty ship in seven and a half minutes to show how yards could do it in 10 days.

Minus its bow, a hull nears completion in a West Coast yard. The largest cranes ever built (background) hoisted the massive prefabricated units into place.

Workers line up to punch out at Kaiser's yard near Portland, Oregon. In shipyards across the United States the day was divided into three eight-hour shifts.

Workers recruited in New York crowd a train station in Hoboken, New Jersey, en route to a Kaiser shipyard in Oregon. Though inexperienced, they were soon welding steel and driving rivets in a race against time.

Ex-waitresses Ina Hickman and May Vincent (left and center) set a shipbuilding record with former seamstress Billie Elliott (right). They welded more plate steel than most of the men who worked at their California yard.

Neatly stacked deck sections and bulkheads for Liberty ships lie ready for hoisting by heavy-duty cranes into hulls taking shape in an Oregon shipyard.

Prefabricated inner-floor sections to go into hull bottoms are stacked four deep, ready to be used.

Welders fix ribs of an inner-floor section in place before adding steel sheathing. These 40-ton sections were assembled only a few feet from the ways.

A massive bulkhead is lowered by a crane into the ribbed hull of a new Liberty ship while welders wait in the bilges, ready to secure it in place.

Only two days on the ways, a hull is ready for its first inner-floor section, which will support heavy cargo loaded into the hold for the Atlantic run.

Workers in Los Angeles clear the way for keel number 150, at left, just after launching the Liberty ship in the background. Yards throughout the country competed to find ways to cut corners; awards and bonuses were given to workers for time-saving ideas.

Beach umbrellas shade welders on stove-hot steel decks of a Liberty ship in the summer sun of Southern California. In spite of occasional scorching days, Kaiser located most of his shipyards in California because of the balmy weather through most of the year.

The stern of a Liberty ship is eased into place by cranes, to be welded to the rest of the vessel. The deck of the ship was then fitted into place.

Topping off the hull, the deckhouse superstructure, including the bridge, is added. Skids will now be greased and the ship will slide down the ways.

President Franklin D. Roosevelt (left) and Kaiser, seated in an open car, watch the launching of the Liberty ship Joseph N. Teal, built in only 10 days.

The wives of four wartime businessmen and industrialists smash bottles of foamy champagne on the bows of newly built Liberty ships. Christenings at this yard in Los Angeles were arranged by Terry Lee, who appears in the background of all these pictures. His job was to make sure the bottle broke, even if he had to help swing it. Kaiser's own wife missed once, and the bottle had to be thrown after the hull.

Working around the clock, Kaiser's busy Oregon shipbuilding yard turns out ships under the glare of floodlights. The three Liberty ships in the foreground

were launched within a single day: one at 12:30 a.m., another at noon, and the third at 4:30 p.m. The midnight christening is shown under way at left.

BIBLIOGRAPHY

Adams, Henry:
   1942: The Year That Doomed the Axis. Paperback Library, 1969.
   Years of Deadly Peril. David McKay Company, Inc., 1969.
Arnold-Forster, Mark, *The World at War.* Stein and Day, 1973.
Baker, Richard, *The Terror of Tobermory.* W. H. Allen, 1972.
Baxter, James Phinney, *Scientists Against Time.* The M.I.T. Press, 1946.
Bekker, Cajus, *Hitler's Naval War.* Doubleday & Company, Inc., 1974.
Brown, Anthony Cave, *Bodyguard of Lies.* Harper & Row, 1975.
Buchheim, Lothar-Günther, *U-Boot Krieg.* R. Piper & Co., 1976.
Bunker, John Gorley, *Liberty Ships: The Ugly Ducklings of World War II.* Naval Institute Press, 1972.
Cant, Gilbert, *The War at Sea.* The John Day Company, 1942.
Chalmers, W. S., *Max Horton and the Western Approaches.* Hodder and Stoughton, 1954.
Churchill, Winston S.:
   The Second World War. Bantam Books.
   Volume I, *The Gathering Storm.* 1974.
   Volume II, *Their Finest Hour.* 1974.
   Volume III, *The Grand Alliance.* 1974.
   Volume IV, *The Hinge of Fate.* 1962.
Creswell, John, *Sea Warfare.* Longmans, Green & Co., 1950.
Davidson, Eugene, *The Trial of the Germans.* The Macmillan Company, 1966.
Dönitz, Karl:
   "The Conduct of the War at Sea," pamphlet published by the U.S. Division of Naval Intelligence, 15 January 1946.
   Memoirs: Ten Years and Twenty Days. The World Publishing Company, 1959.
Eggleston, Wilfrid, *Scientists at War.* Oxford University Press, 1950.
Frank, Wolfgang:
   Enemy Submarine. William Kimber, 1954.
   The Sea Wolves. Rinehart & Company, Inc., 1955.
Gallery, Daniel V., *Clear the Decks!* William Morrow and Company, 1951.
Hough, Richard, *Death of the Battleship.* The Macmillan Company, 1963.
Hull, Cordell, *The Memoirs of Cordell Hull.* Vols. I and II. The Macmillan Company, 1948.
Irving, David, *The Destruction of Convoy PQ.17.* Simon and Schuster, 1968.
Kemp, Peter K., *Key to Victory.* Little, Brown and Company, 1957.
Kennedy, Ludovic, *Pursuit.* The Viking Press, 1974.
King, Ernest J., and Walter Muir Whitehill, *Fleet Admiral King.* W. W. Norton & Company, Inc., 1952.
Lane, Frederic C., *Ships for Victory.* Johns Hopkins Press, 1951.
Langer, William L., and S. Everett Gleason:
   The Challenge to Isolation. Harper & Brothers, 1952.
   The Undeclared War. Harper & Brothers, 1953.
Lash, Joseph P., *Roosevelt and Churchill 1939-1941.* W. W. Norton & Company, Inc., 1976.
Lewis, David D., *The Fight for the Sea.* The World Publishing Company, 1961.
Loewenheim, Francis L., Harold D. Langley, and Manfred Jonas, *Roosevelt and Churchill: Their Secret Wartime Correspondence.* Saturday Review Press/E. P. Dutton & Co., Inc., 1975.
Lund, Paul, and Harry Ludlam:
   Night of the U-Boats. W. Foulsham & Co. Ltd., 1973.
   PQ 17—Convoy to Hell. W. Foulsham & Co. Ltd., 1968.
Macintyre, Donald:
   The Battle of the Atlantic. B. T. Batsford, 1961.
   The Thunder of the Guns. W. W. Norton & Company, Inc., 1959.
   U-Boat Killer. W. W. Norton & Company, Inc., 1956.
MacNeil, Calum, *San Demetrio.* Angus and Robertson, 1957.
Martienssen, Anthony, *Hitler and His Admirals.* Secker and Warburg (London), 1948.
Mason, David, *U-Boat the Secret Menace.* Ballantine Books, 1968.

Mayer, S. L., ed., *Navies of World War II.* The Hamlyn Publishing Group Limited, 1976.
Mohr, Ulrich, *Ship 16.* The John Day Company, 1956.
Monsarrat, Nicholas:
   Breaking In, Breaking Out. William Morrow & Company, Inc., 1971.
   Three Corvettes. Ballantine Books, 1962.
Morison, Samuel Eliot:
   History of United States Naval Operations in World War II. Little, Brown and Company.
   Volume I, *The Battle of the Atlantic.* 1950.
   Volume X, *The Atlantic Battle Won.* 1968.
Noli, Jean, *The Admiral's Wolf Pack.* Doubleday & Company, Inc., 1974.
Parsons, Iaian, ed., *The Encyclopedia of Sea Warfare.* Thomas Y. Crowell Company, 1975.
Pope, Dudley, *The Battle of the River Plate.* William Kimber, 1956.
Potter, E. B., and Chester W. Nimitz, eds., *Sea Power: A Naval History.* Prentice-Hall, Inc., 1960.
Preston, Antony, *An Illustrated History of the Navies of World War II.* The Hamlyn Publishing Group Limited, 1976.
Price, Alfred, *Aircraft versus Submarine.* Naval Institute Press, 1973.
Raeder, Erich, *My Life.* United States Naval Institute, 1960.
Rayner, D. A., *Escort.* William Kimber, 1955.
Reisenberg, Felix, Jr., *Sea War.* Rinehart & Company, Inc., 1956.
Reynolds, Clark G., *Command of the Sea.* William Morrow & Company, Inc., 1974.
Richards, Denis, and Hilary St. George Saunders, *Royal Air Force 1939-1945.* Her Majesty's Stationery Office, 1974.
Robertson, Terence:
   Night Raider of the Atlantic. E. P. Dutton & Co., Inc., 1956.
   Walker, R.N. Evans Brothers, 1956.
Rogers, Stanley, *Enemy in Sight!* Thomas Y. Crowell Company, 1943.
Rohwer, J., and G. Hümmelchen, *Chronology of the War at Sea.* Vol. One: 1939-1942, translated from the German by Derek Masters. Arco Book Publishing Company, Inc., 1972.
Rohwer, Jürgen, *Die U-Boot Erfolge der Achsenmächte 1939-1945.* J. F. Lehmanns, 1968.
Roskill, S. W.:
   The War at Sea (3 vols.). Her Majesty's Stationery Office, 1954-1961.
   White Ensign. United States Naval Institute, 1960.
Schaeffer, Heinz, *U-Boat 977.* W. W. Norton & Company, Inc., 1952.
Seth, Ronald, *The Fiercest Battle.* Hutchinson & Co., Ltd., 1961.
Sherwood, Robert E., *Roosevelt and Hopkins.* Harper & Brothers, 1948.
Shirer, William L.:
   The Rise and Fall of the Third Reich. Simon and Schuster, 1960.
   The Sinking of the Bismarck. Random House, 1962.
Showell, J. P. Mallmann, *U-Boats Under the Swastika.* Ian Allan Ltd., 1974.
Taylor, Telford, *The Breaking Wave.* Simon and Schuster, 1967.
Thursfield, H. G., ed., *Brassey's Naval Annual 1948.* The Macmillan Company, 1948.
Tucker, Gilbert Norman, *The Naval Service of Canada.* King's Printer, 1952.
Von der Porten, Edward P., *The German Navy in World War II.* Thomas Y. Crowell Company, 1969.
Waters, John M., Jr., *Bloody Winter.* D. Van Nostrand Company, 1967.
Watts, Anthony J., *The U-Boat Hunters.* Macdonald and Jane's, 1976.
Williams, E. T., and Helen Palmer, eds., *The Dictionary of National Biography 1951-1960.* Oxford University Press, 1971.
Wilson, Theodore A., *The First Summit.* Houghton Mifflin Company, 1969.
Winn, Godfrey, *P.Q. 17.* Hutchinson & Co., no date.
Winton, John, ed., *The War at Sea 1939-1945.* Hutchinson of London, 1967.
Woodward, David, *The Secret Raiders.* W. W. Norton & Company, Inc., 1955.

ACKNOWLEDGMENTS

The index was prepared by Mel Ingber. The editors also wish to thank William J. Armstrong, Ph.D., History Office, U.S. Naval Air Systems Command, Washington, D.C.; Commander Robert Aubrey, D.S.C., R.N., Ringwood, Hampshire, England; Richard Baker, St. Albans, Hertfordshire, England; Lieselotte Bandelow, Ullstein, Berlin; John D. Barnett, Combat Art Collection, Department of the Navy, Washington, D.C.; Jochen Brennecke, Düsseldorf; Lothar-Günther Buchheim, Feldafing, Germany; R. M. Coppock, Ministry of Defense, Naval Historical Branch, London; Captain Kurt Diggins (Ret.), Director, Deutsches Marine Institut, Bonn-Bad Godesberg, Germany; Grand Admiral Karl Dönitz, Aumühle, Holstein, Germany; Detmar H. Finke, Chief, General Reference Branch, Historical Services Division, Center of Military History, Department of the Army, Washington, D.C.; Ulrich Frodien, Süddeutscher Verlag, Bilderdienst, Munich; Marylou Gjernes, Curator, Center of Military History, Department of the Army, Washington, D.C.; Charles R. Haberlein Jr., Photographic Section, Curator Branch, Naval History Division, Department of the Navy, Washington, D.C.; Commander Stephen Harwood, M.A.R.N., Portsmouth, England; Dr. Matthias Haupt, Bundesarchiv, Koblenz, Germany; Agnes F. Hoover, Photographic Section, Curator Branch, Naval History Division, Department of the Navy, Washington, D.C.; Geraldine Judkins, Operational Archives Branch, Naval History Division, Department of the Navy, Washington, D.C.; Dr. Roland Klemig, Bildarchiv Preussischer Kulturbesitz, Berlin; Judy Koontz, Operational Archives Branch, Naval History Division, Department of the Navy, Washington, D.C.; Charles D. Lawrence, Combat Art Collection, Department of the Navy, Washington, D.C.; William H. Leary, National Archives, Washington, D.C.; Marian McNaughton, Staff Art Curator, Center of Military History, Department of the Army, Washington, D.C.; the staff of the Navy Department Library, Washington, D.C.; Commander the Rt. Hon. Sir Allan Noble, K.C.M.G., D.S.O., D.S.C., Bury St. Edmunds, Suffolk, England; Commodore C. P. C. Noble, C.B.E., D.S.C., V.R.D., R.N.R., London; B. Powell, Ministry of Trade and Industry, London; John C. Reilly, Ships' Histories Branch, Naval History Division, Department of the Navy, Washington, D.C.; Professor Dr. Jürgen Rohwer, Director, Bibliothek für Zeitgeschichte, Stuttgart; Professor Dr. Michael Salewsi, Bonn; David E. Scherman, Stony Point, N.Y.; Commander R. E. Sherwood, D.S.O., R.D., R.N.R. (Ret.), Wendover, Buckinghamshire, England; Nancy Stephenson, Saffron Walden, Essex, England; Rear Admiral Erich Topp (Ret.), Bonn; Jim Trimble, National Archives, Washington, D.C.; Frank Vicovari, Brewster, N.Y.; Captain J. E. Wolfenden, D.S.C., R.D., R.N.R. (Ret.), Etchingham, Kent, England.

PICTURE CREDITS

Credits from left to right are separated by semicolons, from top to bottom by dashes.

INDEX

Printed in U.S.A.